It Only Takes

Top Performers

Ar

Bet

O

T

of Areas

to Have a Competitive Edge in $ales

Thomas A. Freese

Published by
QBS Publishing, Inc.
P.O. Box 922933
Atlanta, Georgia 30010-2933
tfreese@QBSresearch.com

Library of Congress Catalog Card Number: 2001116981

ISBN 13: 978-1-891892-11-0
ISBN 10: 1-891892-11-8

Book design by Jill Dible

Printed in Canada

*This book is dedicated to all
the students who have attended QBS
sales training programs. Thank you for asking
the hard questions and for challenging the
status quo. That's ultimately where
the best ideas come from.*

Acknowledgments

The development of this book, *It Only Takes 1% to Have a Competitive Edge in Sales,* was a team effort. Over the last few years when I was collecting material, and during the many months it took to craft these ideas into one hundred chapters, countless people have contributed to the success of this work—so many that it would be impossible for me to name them individually. But there are several people who deserve special recognition for their support, guidance, and ongoing encouragement. Without them this book would still be a pile of notes on my office credenza.

Much appreciation goes to my executive assistant, Susan Shields, for her commitment to seeing this project through and her patience in putting up with me along the way. Jill Dible deserves special recognition for bringing the pages of this book to life with her creativity and graphic design talents. I also wish to thank Emily Gilreath for her efforts in editing and fine tuning the final transcript.

Special gratitude also goes out to Al Zuckerman, my literary agent in New York; Scott Whitney, my website designer in California; and to several of my best champions, including: Steve Johnson, Richard Sites, Greg Jones, Barry Gillman, Matt Ure, Mark Reed, and Joe Monday. Your continued support and confidence gives me balance and a necessary reality check now and then.

I would also like to thank the early adopters of Question Based Selling for taking a risk and stepping outside the box of traditional sales thinking. For me, it has been a thrill to have the opportunity gain the confidence of companies like Sun

Microsystems, Nortel Networks, KPMG Peat Marwick, Baxter Corporation, Lucent Technologies, Compaq, AOL/Time Warner, Continental Office Furniture, IBM, Shared Medical Systems, 3Com Corporation, GE Capital, Actuate Software, EMC Corporation, Exabyte, VERITAS Software, Clarus Corporation, Resonate Software, and Storage Networks, Inc.

Last but not least, I wish to thank my wife Laura and our two daughters, Sarah and Mary Claire, for allowing me to pursue this dream that keeps getting bigger. You guys will always come first in *my* book.

Table of Contents

Table of Contents

Table of Contents

Preface

Tom Peters and Robert H. Waterman, Jr. changed the face of American business when they wrote the book, *In Search of Excellence*. Before this book was published, corporate managers didn't use phrases like "paradigm shift" or "belief systems," and the now-popular concept of "thinking outside the box" was not something that people even thought about. Essentially, Peters and Waterman initiated the winds of change among corporations, winds that blew with a fervor strong enough to break down many of the barriers that had previously stood in the way of business innovation and cultural progress.

You might say that these two men broke the traditional corporate mold. But it would be more accurate to say that they suggested we take a closer look at our surroundings and break our own molds. As a result, their insights have empowered us to put into practice many important lessons about business. We have realized that being "all dolled up" in expensive pinstripe suits doesn't necessarily make us smarter or more effective than someone else who's wearing an open-collared shirt. We have also learned that while tenure is to be respected, it is not to be revered. Leveraging one's own experiences is valuable, but so is fostering a continuous infusion of fresh ideas. Furthermore, we have learned that a customer-centric focus will withstand the test of time, whereas those people who are inwardly focused, and company-centric, will likely rot on the grapevine of internal politics.

Why am I talking about the winds of change in corporate management? Because, in my opinion, the corporate sales function is ready for a similar "kick in the pants." To me, it's a

1

little ironic that most of the sales training material being delivered today was developed 20+ years ago. I say ironic because I believe the selling environment has changed dramatically in the last twenty years. More companies are offering more solutions than ever before, and their sales forces are being challenged with smaller territories and larger sales quotas. Meanwhile, prospects and customers are being heaped with greater responsibility as their business environments are growing increasingly complex, which leaves them with considerably less time to investigate alternatives and make good business decisions. As a result, the days of sending salespeople out into the field with a smiling face and an outstretched hand are over. Everyone else who is competing with you for a larger share of the market is eager to earn the customer's business too.

What about being more aggressive? That's an idea. But consider this: the next time you receive a telephone call from a salesperson who has decided to be even more "aggressive" with you, does their chances of making a sale go up or down? I'm guessing that if you are like most people that the answer is down!

"Why don't we just keep on teaching salespeople the same stuff that has been taught for the last 20 years?" one might ask. The problem is, teaching salespeople to sound just like everyone else who is targeting the same list of prospect accounts will cause them to forfeit their competitive edge.

Sounding just like everybody else should be the opposite of your objective. If you want to have opportunities to uncover needs and present solutions, you must first be able to differentiate your company, your products, and yourself. Customers today receive dozens of sales calls from countless sales callers, but they will only respond to a few; and only a small fraction of those ever turn into mutually beneficial business relationships. So, what makes a potential buyer take your call as opposed to your competitor's call? Moreover, what makes them want to share their thoughts, feelings, and concerns with you, as opposed to someone else?

Sellers should not be defensive—in fact, just the opposite. Customers all over the world depend on salespeople to provide valuable information and solutions to important problems. They also look to salespeople to help create a vision for success into the future. But they don't depend on every salesperson who comes calling. Building a relationship with every salesperson who calls is simply not feasible. As a salesperson myself, that was fine with me. I did not want my customers to have relationships with everyone. But I did want them to feel that I was one of the salespeople they could depend on.

Perhaps Lee Trevino, the famous professional golfer who won the U.S. Open in 1968, said it best. As he was strolling up the 18th fairway, with a two-stroke lead on the final day of the tournament, Trevino was joking with one of the photographers. This prompted the television announcer to ask him, "Lee, you are competing in one of the biggest golf tournaments of your career, but you don't seem the least bit nervous. Why not?" Trevino casually replied, "Somebody has to win the tournament; it might as well be me."

Well, guess what? Somebody has to win the sale too. Someone has to have a mutually beneficial relationship with the customer. Somebody is going to uncover their needs and then provide valuable solutions. And the customer is going to share their thoughts, feelings and concerns, with somebody—therefore, I say that somebody might as well be you.

Introduction

Sonny Sammons, a friend and fellow author once wrote: "If life was fair, there would be statues of pigeons in our national parks, and dead army generals would periodically come by and poop on them!"

As you know, life is *not* fair. The selling world is not fair either. Look around and you will see that the salesperson with the best product doesn't always win the sale. Likewise, the seller with the most integrity, or who provides the best service after the sale, offers the highest quality, or negotiates the best deal, is no longer guaranteed to win. It's because every salesperson claims to have the best deal, the best service after the sale, and the highest quality. As a result, customers are quick to *commoditize* these similar-sounding claims of greatness, and instead, gravitate toward products, companies, and salespersons who can differentiate themselves in some way.

So, what are you doing to differentiate your products and the company you represent? How can you set yourself apart from all the other sellers who are calling the same list of target accounts?

Ironically, we can no longer depend on our initial training. Even if you have attended many sales training courses in your career, listened to countless cassette tapes, and read all the sales books, the sales environment has changed dramatically over the past few years. Prospects and customers have less time on their calendars to meet with vendors, the overall pace of business continues to quicken, and potential buyers are no longer willing to endure the endless barrage of cold calls from overzealous salespeople.

Sellers used to get extra points for being persistent…but not anymore, as leaving a string of repetitious messages on a prospect's voice-mail system will make you more of a pest than a credible resource. Similarly, it used to be a good strategy for sales managers to send their troops out into the field asking questions to uncover needs. But just because a salesperson wants to ask questions to uncover needs doesn't mean prospects and customers will "want to" share their thoughts, feelings, and concerns. Also, just because a sales professional has a good story, doesn't mean prospects and customers will "want to" hear it. Buyers today don't have the patience or the inclination to spend time with every salesperson who comes along.

Most sellers *can* be excellent resources for providing potential solutions. They can also provide significant value for those customers who are trying to identify potential problems or gather information to make future plans. But only a few salespeople are going to get in the door with their targeted prospect accounts, and even fewer are going to win the business. The question is, do you want to be perceived by customers as "just another salesperson," or would you rather be unique and different?

In my first book, *Secrets of Question Based Selling*, I addressed these issues by introducing Question Based Selling (QBS), a highly-leveraged strategic sales methodology that shows sellers how to engage more prospects in more productive sales conversation throughout the entire sales process. In this book, we build on the concepts of Question Based Selling with a compilation of strategies and selling techniques that you can use to differentiate yourself and your solutions from the rest of the masses. Hopefully, you will find this anecdotal format both enjoyable and easy to read. More importantly, I think you will find that the material inside this book can be implemented immediately with lasting effects that will increase both your confidence and your overall success in sales.

Keep in mind that the margin of victory in sales is usually very small. In fact, the margin of victory in most things is usually quite small. The Kentucky Derby, for example, is almost always won or lost by a fraction of a second. In golf, the smallest variations in the golf swing will ultimately determine whether you score a hole-in-one or hit the ball out-of-bounds. Small margins of victory are found in any competitive environment—especially in sales. If you sell valuable products into a highly competitive marketplace, you must do something to cause prospective buyers to perceive greater amounts of competence, credibility, and value from you, than from your competitors. But you don't need a huge advantage. Most sales are won or lost by very small margins. You simply need an edge—a differentiable advantage that will set you apart from everyone else.

You will find that top performers in sales are not 100% better in any one area of the sales process, rather they are 1% better in hundreds of areas. No matter what industry, the margin of victory at the end of every sale comes from an accumulation of smaller successes that occur throughout the decision cycle. You too can accumulate these smaller successes in order to differentiate your solutions, your company, and yourself from your competition.

When I first started gathering ideas for this book, my goal was not to find the magic bullet. I don't believe in sales gimmicks or closing tricks, and in my view, trying to convince someone to buy something they don't want or need, misses the mark altogether. My goal with this book was simple—to put together a collection of selling strategies and techniques that would give you a 1% advantage in hundreds of areas of the sales process. That's exactly what you will find in the next 100 chapters as we focus on every aspect of the sales process. Therefore, I invite you to buckle your seat belt and get ready for an experience that could change the way you sell. After all, it only takes 1% to have a competitive edge in sales.

Lesson 1
Everyone's a Celebrity

In 1995, my company's sales performance trip was held at the Greenbriar Hotel. All of the salespeople who achieved their quota that year were invited to enjoy the award-winning, Five-Diamond Golf Resort and Spa nestled in the scenic foothills of the Allegheny Mountains in West Virginia.

It didn't take long for my wife Laura and me to acclimate to the luxurious surroundings. After an early morning tee time on the golf links, we enjoyed lunch on the terrace and then headed off to the Greenbriar's world-renowned health spa for a Swedish massage, aromatherapy treatment, and a mud wrap.

We showed up just in time for our 2:00pm appointments. The spa's receptionist politely asked us to wait in the lobby lounge while they notified our assigned therapists that we had arrived. I was called in first. An older man, small in stature, entered the waiting area, introduced himself as "Whitey," and politely invited me to come with him back into the spa's changing area.

Apparently, you don't just get a massage at the Greenbriar Hotel, you get the royal treatment. Whitey first prepared a salt bath in a ten-foot Jacuzzi tub, and put on the CD of my choice. He turned down the lights and promised to return in ten minutes, thus giving me a chance to relax. Of course, ten minutes seemed like two, and then it was time for a Swiss Shower, to rinse off. By the time I finally made it onto the massage table, my body felt like Jell-O.

From previous massage experiences, I knew that it was polite to have some idle conversation during the massage, but

I also knew that the masseur would follow the client's lead. Some people like to be peaceful and quiet. Me, I like to chat.

"How long have you been working here at the hotel?" I asked.

"Since 1958, Mr. Freese," Whitey replied. "Thirty-seven of the best years of my life," he quickly added.

"Wow!" I was duly impressed. Thirty-seven years is a long time.

> "Spending a few minutes to make someone feel special is more significant than spending hours to make them feel average."

The Greenbriar Hotel routinely played host to the rich and famous. In fact, we had already seen several notable television personalities in the lobby. Therefore, my ears perked up when Whitey mentioned that he had recently given a massage to the most successful NFL coach of all time, Miami Dolphins' former head coach, Don Shula.

Wow, again! I couldn't resist the temptation to ask, "Whitey, do you work with a lot of celebrities here at the Greenbriar?"

It was as if he anticipated the question, because Whitey immediately stopped the massage, and with his hands pressed firmly into the small of my back, he calmly replied, "Mr. Freese, every client I give a massage to here at the Greenbriar Hotel is a celebrity!"

How's that for customer service? As I said in my first book, *Secrets of Question Based Selling*, "Spending a few minutes to make someone feel special is more significant than spending hours to make them feel average." With the increasing pace of today's business environment, we could all learn a very important lesson about creating excellent customer satisfaction from Whitey.

Lesson 2
Sometimes it's the Little Things

One of my best successes in the world of large account corporate selling came in 1993, at Nationsbank, now called Bank of America. At the time, I represented NetFrame Systems, a company that manufactured and sold high-end Superservers—large computer hardware that companies used to build massive internal and external local area networks.

Like most high-tech companies, we had plenty of competition, including technology giants like Compaq, IBM, Hitachi, and Hewlett Packard; but our arch-rival in the business was another Superserver manufacturer called Tricord Systems.

At Nationsbank, a heated competitive battle with Tricord for a multi-million dollar server purchase had raged on for nearly six months. When the day came for the contract to be awarded, I received a telephone call in my office from my internal champion at Nationsbank. With noticeable trepidation in her voice, she explained that the decision committee had voted, and it was a tie. A dead heat! Literally, half of the people who were making the decision favored Tricord Systems, and the other half wanted NetFrame.

"Now what?" I asked.

"Are you available next Wednesday?" she replied.

"I can be," I said. "What's going to happen next Wednesday?"

She explained, "In order to break the tie, Nationsbank would like to convene the entire decision committee for a final vendor shoot-out."

"A vendor shoot-out?" I probed.

"Yes. Next Wednesday, we are planning to give Tricord and

11

NetFrame one last opportunity to present to the entire decision committee. During that timeframe, each vendor will have 45 minutes to ask questions or reiterate their benefits, whatever they think will sway the decision." She went on to add, "One vendor will go in the morning and the other in the afternoon, but we only want to hear from one person—the salesperson on the account."

I politely asked if I could go last, so I could leave a lasting impression on the decision-makers. Later that day, I received word that NetFrame would present first in the morning, followed by Tricord in the early afternoon.

At 10:30am the following Wednesday, the Vice President of Information Systems at Nationsbank reintroduced me to the group. For everyone's benefit, he explained that their objective was to break the tie and make a decision later that afternoon after both vendors presented. Then, he handed me the floor of the meeting. Essentially, the stage was set and it was do or die.

The real challenge was, I had already presented our proposed solution to this same audience multiple times. Additionally, I had responded to all their objections and had already addressed any outstanding questions. Therefore, as the salesperson on the account, besides begging for their business, how could I maximize this opportunity for making one last stand?

I opened by thanking the committee for their time and for the opportunity to present one last time. Then I briefly summarized what had occurred to this point in the sale. I asked if anyone had any specific questions. Everyone in the meeting shook their heads, "No." Next, I asked if it would be valuable to hear another product presentation. They shook their heads "No," again. Frankly, it seemed the committee had already decided that either product would meet their needs. If so, the only outstanding question now was which vendor (or perhaps I should say, which salesperson) did they want to do business with?

As I sat there at the end of a huge conference table, it occurred to me that I was still wearing the pager I rented when my wife was pregnant with our first child. Even though our daughter had already been born, I hung on to the pager so my wife could reach me when necessary. I also gave my pager number to select customers, so they could reach me quickly if there was a problem.

Remembering this, I took a shot by making the following plea:

"Ladies and Gentlemen of Nationsbank, we have worked to earn your confidence over the last six months. During that time, we have delivered multiple presentations, and have responded to all your questions. Now we are in a virtual tie. While I am not inclined to beg for your business, I do want to offer you my personal assurance that you will be successful if you decide to choose NetFrame."

Then I stood up, pulled back my suit jacket, and thrust forward the pager that was attached to my belt. Keep in mind that very few salespeople in 1993 wore pagers on their belts. Systems Engineers did, but not salespeople.

"I carry this pager with me all day, every day," I said. *"And if it's not on my belt, it's on the night-stand next to my bed. That's because in addition to providing the most reliable*

computer systems in the industry, NetFrame also provides the highest level of customer service and support. If there's a problem in one of my accounts, I want to know about it!" Then for effect, I added, *"I don't know if the salespeople who work for other competing vendors carry pagers, but if you ever have a problem, you can reach me immediately!"*

With time to spare, I stepped down off my soapbox, exchanged pleasantries with key members of the committee, and the meeting was adjourned.

Later that afternoon, I was nervously pacing back and forth in my office waiting for the telephone to ring. Shortly after four o'clock, my internal champion at Nationsbank called to announce that they had indeed selected a vendor. I felt a certain tightness in my throat as I asked, "Who won?"

"Before I tell you which vendor we selected, I want to share what happened this afternoon during our meeting with Tricord. Much like you," she continued, "the Tricord rep summarized his proposal and reiterated points that had been made over the course of our decision. He also provided a comparison between products. Then, to wrap up the meeting, the Tricord salesperson asked if anyone had any questions."

One hand in the audience shot up like a rocket. It belonged to the Vice President of Information Systems, who asked, "Do you wear a pager?"

"Naaahhh," the Tricord sales rep replied. "My engineer is the one who has to wear the pager."

Guess who was selected vendor of choice? NetFrame! This experience just goes to show that sometimes it's the little things that make the biggest difference.

Lesson 3
The New Competitive Mindset

Two friends were hiking through the woods and stumbled upon a very large grizzly bear. Fiercely, the grizzly reared up on its hind legs and growled. "What should we do?" one friend said, as they now stood face to face with the giant beast. "Run!" yelled the other man. The two friends started running through the woods as fast as they could. With the bear in hot pursuit, one man called out to the other, "How are we going to outrun this bear?" The other man said, "I'm not trying to outrun the bear. I'm trying to outrun you!"

> Winning by a huge margin isn't realistic. It's more likely that you will have a competitive advantage in some areas of the sale and your competitors will have the edge in others.

This wise old parable contains an important lesson about strategic sales. Many sellers go out into their respective territories trying to annihilate their competition in every aspect of the sale. This thinking is flawed because the idea of winning by such a huge margin usually isn't realistic. It's more likely that you will have a competitive advantage in some areas of the sale and your competitors will have the edge in others.

But as we look more closely, we must wonder who your competition actually is? Sure, you have certain arch-rival competitors, the companies and salespeople who are trying to win the business with an alternate solution. But aren't you also competing against the possibility that your prospect may decide to do nothing and maintain the status quo? You may also have to compete against the possibility that prospects will try to solve the problem themselves, rather than purchase your solution. In most opportunities, salespeople not only have to prevail over other competing vendors, they also have to prevail over the possibility of a no-decision, or the possibility that prospects will try to address the problem themselves. This starts to alter the way we must think about our competitors, because oddly enough, your competition in the account is not always your enemy. Sometimes your customer and your competitor are one in the same.

> Salespeople not only have to prevail over other competing vendors, they also have to prevail over the possibility of a no-decision, or the possibility that prospects will try to address the problem themselves.

To be successful in sales, you don't have to destroy your competition, you just have to outrun them. One might say that you have to be willing to go the extra mile. The problem is, in competitive situations, your competitors are trying to go that extra mile too. That's why you must be ready to go the extra mile...plus one inch. And it's that one extra inch that often means the difference between winning and losing the sale. Furthermore, those who sell high-value products or services in a strategic environment must be willing to go the extra mile plus one inch in every aspect of the sales process. That is how top salespeople ultimately broaden their margin of victory. As the subtitle of this book suggests, top performers are not one hundred percent better in any one area of the sale, rather they are one percent better in hundreds of areas.

Lesson 4
"The Best Salesperson I Have Ever Met"

Jim Thanos, Executive Vice President of Worldwide Field Operations for BroadVision, Inc., recently opened his company's national sales meeting with a personal story. Essentially Jim said, "I would like to share a story about the best salesperson I have ever met." This anecdote comes from a real life experience that characterizes what it takes to be successful in sales. Here's Jim's story in a nutshell.

In 1973, Jim Thanos came to the United States from England to join a shared computer services company called National CSS. As part of his ramp up with the company, he was assigned to a mentor named Andrew Abraham.

Andrew Abraham's success at National CSS was legendary. He had over-achieved his sales quota for the past fifteen consecutive years. But as Jim got to know his new mentor, he discovered that success in sales wasn't handed to Andrew. His success came the old fashioned way—he earned it.

Jim learned that Andrew Abraham had immigrated to the United States from Hungary in 1956, during the Hungarian Revolution. With a technical background, he was able to land a job with National CSS as a systems engineer. Andrew was a fine engineer who was content in his position, until he realized that the salespeople at National CSS were making significantly more money than systems engineers. This intrigued Andrew enough that he decided to take action.

The computer industry in the late nineteen-fifties was emerging as the catalyst for change that would eventually lead a virtual industrial re-evolution. Companies that offered shared services, like National CSS, were particularly hot because most customers didn't have the expertise necessary to run their own information systems departments. Therefore, to respond to increasing demand, National CSS was expanding their sales force. When Andrew Abraham learned about this growth, he asked if he could interview for a sales position with the Regional Sales Manager, Peter Yates.

Within moments after Andrew walked into the sales manager's office, Peter Yates knew that the interview needed to be cut short. As you know, first impressions are very important. Well, Mr. Yates' first impression of Andrew had "techno-nerd" written all over it—you know, the stereotypical engineer with high-waisted pants, a plaid shirt that doesn't match, a pocket protector, and an extra helping of brill cream on the hair. Needless to say, Andrew's appearance was not conducive to selling. Peter Yates thanked Andrew for his time, but explained that National CSS was a young company in an emerging market and they were looking for salespeople with more experience.

A few days later, Peter Yates received a letter from Andrew Abraham that was surprisingly upbeat. Andrew thanked Mr. Yates for agreeing to meet with him and reiterated his desire to sell for National CSS. His letter went on to cite examples of people who had faced significant challenges but had persevered until they succeeded. "Did you know that Beethoven was deaf in one ear, and that Wilma Rudolph had epilepsy? Did you know that Winston Churchill failed the sixth grade and that Walt Disney once was fired by a newspaper editor in Los Angeles because he lacked imagination and had no good ideas?" Andrew concluded his letter by saying, "If all I lack is experience, that's an easy obstacle to overcome. Would you consider giving me another opportunity to prove myself?"

Peter Yates kicked Andrew's letter up to his boss, Alan Briggish, the Vice President of Sales. As a result, Andrew was granted a second interview, this time with Mr. Briggish. But just like before, it was obvious very early in the interview that Andrew didn't have the experience that National CSS was looking for in a sales rep.

Rejection didn't stop Andrew. He spent the subsequent weekend putting together a detailed territory plan that included a target account list, a portfolio of ideas for making the sales team more effective, and a timeline showing how he would quickly ramp up in his new sales position. Andrew fronted this territory plan with a professional photograph of himself wearing a dark suit, white shirt, and snappy tie. In the photo, he was holding a briefcase that said, "National CSS Salesperson." Andrew attached a cover letter that read, "Enclosed is a detailed territory plan that should help me and the rest of your sales organization be more successful. This is what I did for you over this past weekend. Imagine what I could do if I worked for you every day!" At the very bottom of his cover letter, Andrew added a post-script saying:

P.S. What did your other salespeople do for you last weekend?

Andrew's letter must have hit a nerve with Alan Briggish because Mr. Briggish forwarded Andrew's package on to Dick Orenstein, President of National CSS, to get his opinion. In a few days, Andrew was summoned to meet with Mr. Orenstein for yet another interview.

Getting right to the point, Mr. Orenstein said, "Mr. Abraham, it is critical at National CSS that our salespeople be able to penetrate into the executive level within our target accounts. Therefore, Andrew, without any formal sales training or experience, how would you be able to get in front of the CEO at Pan Am, for example?"

Andrew paused for a moment and then said, "Over the last few weeks, I have pursued a sales position at National CSS much like I would pursue an opportunity at Pan Am—and without any formal sales training or experience, I succeeded in getting in front of you."

As you may have already guessed, Andrew Abraham was offered a sales position at National CSS. Peter Yates became his first sales manager and Andrew went on to become one of the most successful computer salesman in the early days of technology sales.

There's a lesson in this story that starts with this very simple question. What did you do for your boss (or your customer) last weekend?

Lesson 5
Sellers Must Rise Above "The Noise"

Today, customers are being deluged with sales calls, advertisments, and sponsorship requests, and there is now a tremendous amount of "noise" in the technology, manufacturing, telecommunications, healthcare, transportation, education, energy, and financial services marketplaces. Perhaps this should be no surprise since there are more companies offering more products and services than ever before. As a result, if the solutions you offer are not appropriately differentiated, your value proposition will get lost in the daily noise.

To be successful in today's selling environment, you must rise above the noise. That is ultimately how you gain the competitive advantage necessary to differentiate your products, your company, and most importantly, yourself.

For many sales organizations, this issue of having to rise above the noise has become one of their biggest challenges. But the amount of noise in today's marketplace doesn't have to be your enemy. The fact that it is getting tougher to penetrate new accounts can actually help you. It's simple really. If you succeed in differentiating yourself and your solutions from other vendors, your perceived value will increase, while your competitor's messages, who all tend to sound very much the same, will continue to get lost in the noise.

Lesson 6
Why "Sales 101" No Longer Works

Whenever I kick off a sales training or speaking engagement, I usually poll the audience to find out how many previous sales trainings the group has been through. "Raise your hand," I'll say, "if you have attended two or more sales training courses thus far in your professional career." Most everyone in the audience raises their hands. "Now, keep your hands up if you've attended five or more sales training courses in your career." In many cases, the majority of the audience keeps their hands raised. Then, I ask, "How many of you would like to never have to attend another sales training class ever?" Everyone laughs (and they keep their hands up!). "Me too," I say, and I mean it. In fact, when I left the corporate world in 1996, I remember thinking that I would go nuts if I had had to sit through one more sales training course.

> Most of the sales training material currently being offered was developed 20+ years ago, but the selling environment has changed dramatically over the past twenty years.

When I accepted my first position as a salesperson, I didn't know how to sell. I just assumed that to be successful in sales, all you had to do was ask lots of questions and present valuable solutions. Little did I know, selling wasn't that easy. Consequently, the standard sales 101 training classes I went through served the very important function of teaching me the basics.

I read all the sales books I could get my hands on and I also listened to countless audiocassette tapes about selling. Meanwhile each of the companies I sold for put all of its salespeople through a training regiment designed to get new salespeople up to speed.

It didn't take long, however, before I had been through most of the name brand sales training courses—programs like Strategic Selling, Power Base Selling, Solution Selling, PSS, SPIN Selling, Integrity Selling, and Target Account Selling. Trust me, I've been through them all!

Were these programs helpful? Yes! Each of these training curriculums had unique kernels of wisdom that I found useful. But as I said earlier, it's ironic to me that most of the sales training material currently being offered was developed 20+ years ago. The sheer age of this material poses several challenges for sales managers, starting with the fact that the sales environment has changed dramatically over the past twenty years. It's very difficult to energize a veteran sales force with the same old, same old. Additionally, sales managers know that most of their competitors have attended these same sales training courses too. As a result, teaching salespeople to sound just like everyone else who is calling on the same list of target accounts, forfeits their competitive edge.

The complexity that is being built into some of these programs is another issue. Of the training programs mentioned above, several are documentation intensive—where salespeople are supposed to go out into their respective territories and document the details of every sales conversation onto large detailed spreadsheets. While capturing the details of every account is a noble goal, it's dangerous to assume that increasing a salesperson's administrative responsibilities will make them more productive. Furthermore, just because a salesperson wants to fill in their spreadsheets does not mean prospects and customers will want to share information about their opportunity. In fact, what would make customers want to share account information with you as opposed to the other forty or fifty salespeople who are asking similar questions, wanting to fill in the blanks on their account management profiles?

Perhaps the detail we are trying to capture is missing the mark altogether. Most sales training courses are intended to make *the salesperson* more effective. But if you are selling into corporate markets, for example, there is a good chance that you are *not* the true salesperson on the account. More than likely, you will be dealing with multiple decision-makers, key influencers, and executive sponsors. When this occurs, perhaps we should take a step back and ask, who is the real salesperson in the account?

How much formal sales training have your internal champions had in their careers?

Have you ever noticed that most strategic decisions at large corporate accounts are made behind closed doors? After the parties to the decision have investigated different alternatives, they congregate in a meeting to weigh their options and come to a decision. Therefore, to succeed in making a sale, somebody in these meetings (i.e. your internal champion) must be selling for you, or with you. To win the sale, your internal champion must be willing to carry your flag up the proverbial hill and recommend that others should also buy into your product or service. Thus, the argument can be made that these internal champions are the real salespeople in your accounts. So, here's the tough question. How much formal sales training have your internal champions had in their careers? The answer is, probably not very much. Now the question is: What are you doing to increase the effectiveness of your internal champions to make them better "flag carriers" when they are trying to sell your product or service internally?

Every time I deliver a QBS training program, someone in the audience asks, "Tom, what caused you to go into strategic sales training?"

My answer is always the same. "As a salesperson, I was bored with the same old... same old. I had already been through all the standard sales training courses, and I had endured all the sales *hype* I could stand. What I wanted was a proven sales methodology that could increase my strategic effectiveness and differentiate my value throughout the entire sales process.

That's why I created Question Based Selling!"

I should make the point that while I was in corporate sales, one of the reasons I was able to consistently oversell my sales quota was because I spent little time thinking about who I was selling "to," and instead focused more on who I was selling "through." Empowering others to be more effective carriers of your value messages will translate into increased sales results. That is why building better champions is a primary focus throughout this book, as it was in *Secrets of Question Based Selling.*

Lesson 7
Have You Ever Met Pierre?

A newly hired woodchopper named Pierre arrived in the forest for his first day on the job. Pierre was a strapping young man who could chop wood faster than anyone else in the company. His steadfast endurance enabled him to maintain a feverish pace while chopping wood all day long.

By the end of the first day, however, all of the other woodchoppers had finished chopping their piles of wood, but not Pierre. That was strange since Pierre seemed to be working much harder than everyone else.

One of the older and more experienced wood choppers called over to him, saying, "Hey Pierre, you might want to try sharpening your axe."

Pierre replied, "I don't have time to stop and sharpen my axe. I need to finish chopping all this wood."

Get it? Pierre's story sounds all too familiar in the world of professional sales. How many salespeople go out into their respective territories and labor all day long without ever taking time out to sharpen their sales skills? I know it can be difficult to think strategically when things get fast and furious, but if you want to be successful in sales, you must not lose perspective. In addition to being steadfast and persistent, you must also be effective in your efforts. This includes stopping long enough to assess your strategic selling skills and then developing a plan that will vault you ahead of the competition.

So, let me ask, "Have you ever met Pierre?" Perhaps it would be even more poignant to hold up a mirror and see if there is a little bit of Pierre inside each one of us. If so, maybe it's time to start sharpening your sales skills.

Lesson 8
Curiosity: The Genesis of Every Sale

Whenever I strategize with sales executives about their business, I always ask, "What are your salespeople doing to leverage curiosity in the sales process?" The most common answer I hear is, "Huh?" Then they ask, "What do you mean by leveraging curiosity?"

To me, it's ironic that traditional sales training programs spend so much time stressing the importance of penetrating new accounts, but they don't talk about the importance of leveraging curiosity in the sales process. If you step back from the daily grind and take a strategic look, you will begin to notice that curiosity is the genesis of every sale. Until a prospect becomes curious about who you are or what you can do for them, you will not have an opportunity to uncover their needs or present your solutions.

> Until a prospect becomes curious about who you are or what you can do for them, you will not have an opportunity to uncover their needs or present your solutions.

People tend to prioritize things based on their level of interest. As a result, prospects and customers who become curious, about who you are or what you can do for them, are much more likely to make time for you than someone who is not the least bit curious.

Curiosity is a very powerful human emotion. People naturally focus their time and attention on those things that they are curious about, while all the other things that do not grab their attention fade into the background. Test it out for yourself. The easiest way to make someone curious is to simply say, "Hey, guess what?" After you say this, watch their reaction. Virtually everyone will respond the same way, saying, "What?" But the true test of someone's curiosity is not in what they say, it's in their eyes. If you say to someone, "Guess what?", and then observe their reaction, they will turn toward you, their eyes will widen, and at that very moment in time, you will have their complete attention. This reaction happens because curiosity causes people to focus their attention on whatever they are most curious about.

I am not suggesting that sellers should go out into their respective territories and start calling prospective customers saying, "Guess what?" But I am suggesting that if you try this experiment, and you consciously recognize that curiosity is indeed a very powerful human emotion, then you will start to leverage it in the sales process, which will increase the amount of mindshare you will get from prospects and customers, and enhance your sales results.

How can you leverage curiosity in the sales process? In my first book, *Secrets of Question Based Selling*, we examined this topic extensively. While there is no point in reinventing the wheel here, I do want to highlight some of the key points in the sales process where curiosity can give you a significant advantage.

When Leaving Voice-Mail Messages

If you ask key decision-makers in the corporate world how many voice-mail messages they receive from salespeople in a typical month, they will probably say, "A lot!" or "Hundreds!"

Next, if you ask them if they ever return any of these voice-mail messages left by sales callers, most will admit that they do respond to some messages, but overall, they call very few salespeople back.

Lastly, if you ask these decision-makers what causes them to respond to this small fraction of sales callers, they will say that something grabbed their attention or sparked their interest, which prompted them to return the call. Essentially, something on the voice-mail message made them curious.

The formula for leaving effective voice-mail messages is relatively simple. If a prospect become curious about something you said in your voice-mail message, they will return your call. It's one of the great secrets in selling. It's also one of the reasons top performers are able to consistently overachieve their sales objectives. When I leave voice-mail messages for new prospects, my call back rate is very high. That's because when I leave voice-mail messages, I don't think about features, benefits, problems, solutions, new announcements, or industry trends. Instead, I think about only one thing—what can I say, or what voice-mail message can I leave, that will cause this person to become curious enough to call me back?

Using Email to Your Advantage

Email is similar to voice-mail in the sense that people prioritize their messages based on their level of interest. Therefore, much like voice-mail, prospects and customers who become curious about the email messages you've sent will choose to engage, while those who are not curious won't. Given the hustle and bustle of today's business world, you have to grab someone's attention so that your messages will be prioritized ahead of the many other messages they receive. This is particularly important when sending email because people tend to respond more robustly to those messages that get opened first.

The key to leveraging curiosity in an email message is in the subject field. When prospective customers download their email messages, three fields appear on the screen—date, sender, and subject. The date and sender fields are assigned automatically. The person sending the message, however, enters the subject field. Its purpose is to grab the recipient's attention so they will hopefully become curious enough to open the email message and engage further. This is essentially what newspapers do when they put provocative headlines on the front page in order to grab the reader's attention.

What can you put into the subject field to grab your prospect's attention? The possibilities are endless. Suppose, for example, you want to send an email to follow up on a recent meeting with a new prospect. You could just tell the prospect what your message is about by inserting a standard phrase into the subject field—like, *Following up on yesterday's meeting.* In my mind, standard subject phrases like this one aren't as likely to grab the prospect's attention as something more creative— perhaps a subject line like:

Message to: linda.murphy@XYZcompany.com

From: Tom Freese

Date: April 9, 2001

Subject: Here's Another Idea...

Linda,

Thanks for your time last Thursday morning. It was certainly a pleasure meeting with you and I appreciate hearing about your company's upcoming merger plans. Since October is rapidly approaching, I would suggest that we take a few days to formulate a preliminary migration plan and then get together next week to review. Are you available next Monday afternoon for a meeting or conference call? If not, here's another idea. What about meeting Wednesday for lunch?

Let me know what works best for you.

-Tom

If the subject phrase, "Here's Another Idea..." causes your prospect to become curious about what your idea is, they will immediately open your email. Inducing prospect curiosity using the subject field is a powerful technique. But I must caution you on two fronts. First, you must be sure that your email messages don't look like SPAM. As email messaging has become more popular, the amount of junk email (i.e. SPAM) on the Internet has increased significantly. Therefore, your messages will not be taken seriously if your subject field sounds too sales-y, like: ***WONDERFUL OPPORTUNITY FOR YOU TODAY!***

Secondly, it's important that the phrase you put in the subject field is congruent with your actual message. The easiest way to accomplish this is to enter the subject field last. Type your email message first. Then read it carefully. Three or four different phrases in the body of your message will stick out as potential ticklers that can easily be plugged into the subject field to induce the prospect's curiosity and cause them to read your message. In the sample message above, I chose the phrase, *"Here's another idea…"* as my subject, but I could just as easily have used, *"October is rapidly approaching…"* or *"Your upcoming merger plans…"* as other curiosity-inducing subjects.

Getting to Higher Levels Within Your Accounts

The most effective way to escalate the sale to higher levels within your corporate accounts is to make high level people more curious about what you can do for them. The reason we want to get to higher levels within large corporate accounts is because we want to be dealing with people who have the budget and the authority to make a decision. We also want to get to the person who has the ability to get others involved who will need to facilitate the actual purchase. Therefore, it is to your advantage to involve higher-level decision-makers early in the decision cycle so they can become active participants throughout the rest of the sales process.

Ironically, many salespeople spend much of their time trying to satisfy a top executive's curiosity. In an attempt to communicate value, sellers spew forth information in the hope that this will increase their chances of making a sale. But rather than trying to satisfy your executive's curiosity, perhaps we should ask: What will make top executives curious enough to become personally involved? More than likely, the catalyst that sparks their interest will be the realization that you, or the solutions you offer, can help them in some significant way. For example, suppose you said to an executive, "Over the past two months, we have talked with a number of your divisions who are very excited about our solutions. But I am concerned that we aren't addressing the bigger problem. If we look at this from an enterprise viewpoint, I think we could reduce your expenditures by twenty-five percent and increase your company's revenue projections in the process. Therefore, I wanted to contact you directly to see if it would make sense for us to have a more strategic conversation?" The realization that they might benefit by talking with you is the catalyst that will stimulate additional conversation.

Making Your Audiences More Receptive

As sellers get excited about their respective value propositions, they tend to believe that their ideas will stand on their own merit. But this thinking often misses the larger opportunity. Just because you have a good idea doesn't mean your prospects and customers will be receptive to hearing it.

How do you make people more receptive to your ideas? The answer is, you leverage their curiosity. Suppose you are in the midst of a sales call, for example, and you are making points regarding how your solutions could increase the prospect's productivity. If you want to transition the conversation to other areas where your product or service might add value, you can say, "Mr. Prospect, productivity is important, but I have some other thoughts about how our solutions would help your business. Would you like to hear my ideas?"

If you pique the prospect's curiosity with something that is relevant and important to their business, of course they will want to hear more. In addition to making potential buyers more receptive, leveraging curiosity is also an excellent technique for expanding your opportunity to provide value.

Dangling Incentives That Will Close the Sale

Curiosity is also a powerful strategy when trying to close a sale. For years, it has been common practice for sellers to dangle special incentives or discounts in front of their prospects, hoping that these incentives will entice buyers to move forward with a purchase. Too often, however, sales are squandered because the impact of the incentive being offered gets lost in the delivery. For example, in an attempt to close a deal, a salesperson might ask, "If we give you an additional 15% discount, would you be willing to make a decision today?" If the salesperson doesn't know whether this discount is something that will motivate the prospect or not, offering it puts them in a weak position by giving away too much without asking for something in return. Unfortunately, buyers tend to be even more stand-offish once they have all the information they need to make a purchase decision.

I would much rather use curiosity as an incentive that causes prospects to want to engage further. Therefore, rather than just throwing out discounted numbers, my strategy is to use curiosity to secure a commitment first, by asking, "Mr. Prospect, if you are close to making a decision, we would like to offer you an incentive to wrap this sale up by the end of the month. Therefore, I wanted to ask if it would make sense for us to have this conversation?"

Just by mentioning the possibility of additional discounts, most prospects will immediately want to know more. This puts you in a position of strength where you can appropriately qualify the opportunity before specifying any incentives you might be able to offer.

Summary Point

Leveraging curiosity in the sales process is not some gimmick for deceiving customers, nor is it a way to trick them into spending time with you. Rather, curiosity is the genesis of every sale. It's simple really. Curious prospects will choose to engage in a productive conversation about their needs and your value, while those prospects who are not curious won't.

Curiosity is also a catalyst that propels the sales process forward. The more curious your prospects become, the deeper and broader they will want to engage. Given that curiosity is such an important ingredient in a salesperson's success, don't you think it's strange that other sales programs don't talk about leveraging curiosity throughout the sales process?

At a recent speaking engagement, a Director of Marketing pulled me aside and asked, "With the success of Question Based Selling, do you think you will be remembered as the sales trainer who invented curiosity?"

"I didn't invent human behavior," I said. "I have just observed people long enough to realize that what motivates them to *want to* engage often contradicts what has been preached in traditional sales methods for many years. Essentially, I just lifted up the rug and pointed at the dirt." I would much rather be the sales trainer who points to the real challenges in today's selling environment and teaches salespeople how to more effectively differentiate themselves using "non-traditional" methods. With that said, let me ask, what are you doing to leverage curiosity in your sales opportunities?

Lesson 9
Earning the Right to Succeed

Tom Malchow captured an Olympic Gold Medal for the United States at the 2000 Summer Olympic Games by winning the Men's 200-meter Butterfly in Sydney. When he was interviewed after the race, one of the announcers shoved a microphone in his face and asked him about the victory. Tom's response was interesting. He said, "Leading up to the games in Sydney, I worked harder than ever because I wanted to be able to look to my left, and then to my right at the start of the race, knowing that I had earned the right to succeed."

When I first started out in sales, I had to kick, scratch, and claw to make any headway. Every sale was a battle, and in each opportunity, I felt like the underdog. Perhaps it was because I had relatively little selling experience at the time, or maybe it was just because I didn't descend from a long line of genetically gifted salespeople. Whatever the reason, I found it overwhelming to always feel like an under-achiever.

Fortunately, people respond to pressure in different ways. Some people, when they start to feel overwhelmed, fade into the background, not wanting to bring attention to the fact that they are struggling. As for me, increased pressure tends to make me more indignant. If I am going to fail at something, I would rather go down in flames.

On January 1, 1988, I made a career changing New Year's resolution. I had just finished up a mediocre sales year and damn it, I wasn't going to have another one. So I headed to the office. While everyone else nursed their post New Year's Eve hangovers and watched college football, I cleaned out my desk and got seriously organized. I worked the entire day. It was no surprise that mine was the only car in the parking lot since it was a holiday. But by the time I left the office, I felt a very clear sense of satisfaction and preparedness. I was ready for the New Year.

Have you ever noticed how good it feels to be ahead of the game? For the entire first week of January, while everyone else was trying to catch up, I was moving forward and feeling productive. In fact, it felt so good that I was motivated to stay ahead. Consequently, I often remained at the office late into the evening and came in frequently on weekends, each time noticing that mine was the only car in the parking lot.

My strategy was simple. I was determined to outwork everyone else on the sales team. That way, if I did fail, I wouldn't have any excuses. Besides working longer hours, I also made it a goal to work harder than everyone else. I made more cold calls than other salespeople and scheduled the most appointments. I also asked the most questions in order to uncover more needs. I even made it a point to take the most notes at every meeting. After a very short period of time, my extra effort caused me to become significantly more knowledgeable about our product offerings and target industry, which in turn, made me a much more credible resource to my prospects and customers. As the year progressed, I began to feel less overwhelmed and more in control.

It didn't take long before I became the "go to" guy in the office. When someone had a question, they came to me for help. And when the sales manager had a new opportunity, he sent it my way, knowing that it would be handled more thoroughly and with a greater sense of urgency. By year-end, I had become the top producing salesperson in the office. Essentially, I had earned the right to outperform everyone else whose car wasn't parked in the lot on that New Year's Day.

> If you view yourself as an average performer, you most likely will be.

Now, I'm not saying you should work every holiday or abandon your family by "living" at the office. Too much of anything is bad. What I am saying, though, is that for me, increasing my commitment raised my knowledge level and my self-confidence, which completely changed my perspective.

The perception you have about your own abilities will greatly influence your probability of success in sales. If you view yourself as an average performer, you most likely will be. On the other hand, if you put yourself in a position to overachieve, then you will likely see some very powerful results from your extra efforts.

Lesson 10
Shorten Your Ramp-Up Window

When I first started with NetFrame Systems, Inc., I didn't know much about computer hardware. I had been selling software and services for years, but someone else always worried about the hardware platform. Therefore, I needed to find a way to ramp up quickly in order to learn all the different aspects of a local area network.

NetFrame held four-day boot camps at their corporate headquarters in the Silicon Valley where newly hired salespeople would come out for a Tuesday through Friday orientation, to learn the basic NetFrame sales pitch. So that I could learn more about the hardware platform itself, I arranged to arrive early and spend a day with Ric Tappero, NetFrame's lead pre-sales engineer at the time. Ric was kind enough to give me a personal lesson in computer hardware.

Ric didn't know what he was getting himself into. I was such a novice with respect to computers that he ended up answering questions like, "What is a mother board?" "How do you plug the machine into a customer's network?"…and… "How does an Intel processor work?"

As the conversation grew more technical, I asked if it would be possible to open up a NetFrame and examine its component parts. Ric obliged and we started removing parts from an actual system. The drill was simple. Ric pulled out a component and I asked detailed questions about it. He held up an I/O processor, for example, and I pointed to the various electronic components on the board and asked questions like, "What are these little yellow things that looks like M&Ms?"

"Those are 50 Ohm resisters," Ric answered.

"What are they for?" I continued.

"You don't need to know that," Ric explained.

"Indulge me, I'm curious," I would say.

Ric answered all my questions, but he kept saying that I didn't need to know this much technical detail. But I wanted the details, so we spent the rest of the day examining the system, component by component. By the time we finished, we had literally disassembled a NetFrame and put it back together again.

> "This new sales guy from Atlanta is a lunatic! He thinks he wants to be a Systems Engineer!"

That night, Ric telephoned my new boss in Philadelphia saying, "This new sales guy from Atlanta is a lunatic! He thinks he wants to be a Systems Engineer!" I spent the rest of the week learning the NetFrame presentation like the other sales reps. Then we all headed back into our respective territories to put what we learned to good use. Time would tell how productive the training had been.

Between you and me, I never had any desire to be a Systems Engineer. But I did want to arm myself with lots of information so I wouldn't sound ignorant in front of live customers. Actually, I just wanted to accumulate a base of knowledge and have a few facts that could boost my credibility, knowing that I wouldn't always have the answer to other important questions. (Frankly, it's a little embarrassing if you don't know anything about your product.) I wanted to be able to demonstrate at least some knowledge so prospects would be more forgiving with my other areas of inexperience.

Case in point: The week after I returned from NetFrame's boot camp, I encountered a prospect who wanted to play 'stump the chump.' You know the type, where an engineer from the customer tries to test a salesperson's mettle by asking detailed questions to expose how much you don't know.

This particular prospect opened the conversation with an ultra-detailed technical question about the electronic integrity of our systems, and frankly, I had no idea how to respond. I didn't even understand his question well enough to restate it. I was definitely stumped. So I said, "I don't know how to answer your question. However, I can tell you how many screws hold the motherboard of a NetFrame onto its chassis, because I've taken an entire system apart with a screwdriver." I added, "If you can help me understand more about your specific question and why it is important, I will get back to you with the answer."

Since Ric and I had taken apart a fully assembled NetFrame, I knew some impressive trivia about our hardware. Having these facts helped me compensate for the reality that I didn't know everything. The prospect started to loosen up almost immediately. He got an opportunity to demonstrate his depth of knowledge and I had an opportunity to demonstrate mine. As it turned out, we both knew stuff the other didn't. As a result, we exchanged some technical factoids and bonded instantly. It was clear that my time with Ric had been well spent.

There's an important lesson here. My goal in meeting with Ric was to increase my confidence by increasing my hands-on knowledge of what I was selling. I didn't want to be talking with customers about Superservers without ever having seen the inside of one. While this may sound intuitive, you would be amazed how many salespeople I meet who haven't ever broken the shrink-wrap on the products they sell.

My strategy at NetFrame paid huge dividends by allowing me to ramp-up much more quickly than anyone had previously. The reward was finishing 300% of my sales quota in only my second quarter with the company.

Lesson 11
Let Us Solve Your Most Difficult Business Problem

International Network Services (INS) was acquired by Lucent Technologies in November of 1999, after exploding into a multi-hundred million-dollar company specializing in high-end network professional services. Five years earlier, INS was only a start-up venture, working hard to carve out a niche for the delivery of advanced technical support and design services for corporate customers who wanted to leverage the power of computer networks as part of their information systems strategy.

Early on, INS's sales force went out into the field pounding on doors, just like any other start-up venture. Essentially, they went around telling prospects about their technical superiority and unique engineering capabilities. But INS struggled when trying to differentiate themselves because they were only one of many companies that offered technical services at the time, and everybody else was claiming they were great too!

As a strategy to penetrate more new accounts, INS started

making the following offer: "Give us your most difficult networking problem, the one that keeps you up at night. We will address that problem first. Then if, after a reasonable period of time, we are not able to solve your most difficult problem, you pay nothing for our services."

This was a powerful offer. For an information systems manager, INS's offer to solve their most difficult problem created a powerful vision where one of their biggest challenges could suddenly disappear without any risk to them or their operations. If INS succeeded, the manager would look like a hero for bringing in the appropriate technical resources. If not, INS was willing to incur the cost of their time and effort.

Ironically, this offer was a no-risk strategy for INS as well. Once a prospective customer accepted INS's offer, the next step was to sit down with the technical staff in the account and understand the customer's "most difficult problem." This strategy session gave the INS sales team an opportunity to assess the customer's technical environment. It also gave them an opportunity to qualify the legitimacy of the project. If the customer's most difficult problem was indeed solvable, INS would quote a price for their services and then make the problem go away. Of course, this was a win/win situation. By solving the customer's most difficult problem, the INS team was able to gain the customer's confidence, which created all kinds of other opportunities to provide engineering services and technical support in the future.

Sometimes in these technical meetings, it became clear during the assessment that the customer's most difficult problem was not solvable. When this occurred, INS would respectfully decline, but this forum still gave them a wonderful opportunity to demonstrate their technical prowess by explaining the complexity of the problem and helping the customer identify other possible alternatives. Another win/win. Even when INS wasn't able to solve the customer's most difficult problem, they were able to establish relationships with customers and gain credibility as a valuable technical resource. Best of all, when the customer became stumped by another difficult problem in the future, guess who they would call for help? Terrific penetration strategy!

Lesson 12
The Phrase That Pays

I am not a big fan of trying to script a specific dialogue for salespeople. Those who do try to implement a scripted approach usually find that their actual conversations with "live" prospects quickly veer away from the script. Live sales conversations are dynamic in nature and every opportunity is different. Therefore, I hold the opinion that it's much more productive and fruitful to develop a set of mental templates that can be used to manage your sales conversations, from the initial contact to closing on appropriate next steps in the sale. While there aren't any magic words that will cause people to buy goods and services they don't want, there are certain "money phrases" that can increase your probability of success.

Take the initial sales call, for example. When contacting new prospects, it's important to have a good opening line. But so many opening lines in today's business environment are scripted to sound too "sales-y." To avoid this, when I talk with new prospects, I introduce myself and then say:

> **Salesperson:** "Mr. Prospect, I was hoping to catch you for a minute to discuss (insert legitimate reason for calling). Did I happen to catch you at a bad time?"

If you have a legitimate reason for calling (perhaps to discuss issues related to an upcoming meeting), the phrase, "I was hoping to catch you for a minute," and the question, "Did I happen to catch you at a bad time?", are particularly effective. They sound down-to-earth and respectful of the other person's time, which tends to lower the prospect's defenses. If you are calling about something that piques their interest, most will respond by giving you a few minutes. If you do happen to catch someone at a bad time, like when they are running off to a meeting, you can simply say, "When should I call you back?" Once again, to the extent that you have a legitimate reason for calling, prospects will give you a specific time when they expect to be more available. Now you have an appointment.

> While there aren't any magic words that will cause people to buy something they don't want, there are certain "money phrases" that can increase your probability of success.

Another strategy to use when kicking off your sales conversations with new prospects is to open with a legitimate reason for calling, and then follow up with a "money phrase" like, "…so I picked up the telephone to see if it would make sense for us to have a conversation." If we surround this phrase with some real life verbiage, the conversation might sound like:

> **Salesperson:** "Mr. Prospect, we just completed some engineering studies in your Chicago and Dallas offices which resulted in productivity increases of more than 50%. Brian Gibson, your counterpart in Chicago, thought we might be able to deliver the same benefits for your operation…so I picked up the telephone to see if it would make sense for us to have a conversation."

Once again, this is a high percentage play. If you have a legitimate reason for calling (and a productivity increase of 50% is definitely legitimate), of course it "makes sense" to have a conversation.

Dealing with the Right Person

After first engaging a new prospect, I usually follow up with a qualifying question to make sure that I am dealing with the right person. There's no magic here. I simply ask: "Are you the person who handles _____? " Or, "Are you the person I should be talking with about _____?"

If they respond by saying, "Yes, that's me," they have given their implied permission to proceed with a more specific conversation about the topic at hand. If whoever you are talking with is not the appropriate person, then this phraseology will usually cause them to tell you who is.

After you succeed in getting past the opening line, and you have the right person on the telephone, what happens next? Throughout the QBS Methodology, I stress the importance of asking good questions, knowing that sellers must first identify potential needs in order to have opportunities to communicate value. The easiest way to transition your conversations into discovery is with this simple phrase: "Can I ask a question about your business?" If you have a legitimate reason for calling and you have earned the right to take the conversation to the next level, most prospects will respond by saying, "Sure." Of course, if you ask an intelligent question, you earn the right to ask another...and another.

Use Humility for Best Results

Some of the most productive questions a salesperson can ask include "money phrases" like, "Can you help me understand...," or, "I'm confused about..." Remember, we have already found that not knowing every detail is OK, so humble phrases like these invite prospects to come to your rescue, and they do so by sharing more information. Most people feel good about helping others. Therefore, why not make them feel good about helping you understand more about their needs?

When the initial conversation is going along well, sellers need to look for opportunities to move the sales process forward. When closing for an on-site meeting, for example, I leverage a familiar phrase saying, "If these are the issues you face, and that's how we provide value to customers, would it make sense for us to schedule an on-site meeting, so we can have a more in-depth discussion?" Again, the phrase, "would it make sense to…" is very down to earth and non-threatening, thereby making it easy for prospects to say, "Yes." The next question I ask is, "Do you happen to have your calendar handy?"

When you do succeed in securing the follow-up meeting, don't hang up. Your job has just begun. After selecting a time and date for the meeting, you should also ask, "Who else needs to be involved?" The last thing you want is to have one or more key players in the decision absent from this meeting because the prospect didn't think to invite them.

Techniques That Will Open the Floodgates

During your sales conversations, it's critical to know what prospects and customers are thinking relative to where they stand on the various issues being discussed. But unless you are a mind reader, you cannot know without asking. The tough part is, just because we would like their input or feedback doesn't necessarily mean prospects will want to share with you. This is where a little strategy and technique can go a long way.

One way to find out what your prospects and customers are thinking is to be direct, asking, "How do you feel about _____?" Prospects who are already comfortable with you will share their thoughts, feelings and concerns.

When customers are more tentative about sharing, a more creative way to solicit feedback in your sales opportunities is to probe for potential unrest by asking, "Is there anything you would change about our proposal, or our approach thus far?" Or, since people like to be asked for their opinion, you can be even more direct by asking, "If you were the salesperson on this account, how would you handle _____?"

One of my favorite feedback strategies is to take the conversation off the record. At the appropriate time in a conversation, I might say, "Mr. Prospect, can I ask you something…off the record? How does senior management really feel about our proposed solution?" I don't know who's actually keeping a record, but so long as you are off it, it's amazing how much valuable information prospects and customers will share.

Ask Your Prospects to Help Predict the Future

Sometimes, the best way to ask for feedback is the simplest way. Therefore, one of the most powerful phrases to use when soliciting feedback from prospective customers is to simply ask, "Where do we go from here?" People always appreciate that you are interested in their opinion, and this simple phrase is a non-threatening way to find out where you stand in the sale.

A similar technique would be to ask, "Mr. Prospect, what do you think should happen next?" It's important to remember that they too have a stake in the outcome of the sale, so you might as well ask their opinion.

Empathy is a Powerful Bonding Tool

One of the most powerful phrases sellers have at their disposal is also one of the most universal—saying, "I understand how you feel." Even in the sales arena, being empathetic towards another person's needs or concerns can be more valuable than actually solving the problem. Don't just take my word for it. Any psychologist or family counselor will tell you that most relationship problems are the result of someone who becomes frustrated because their partner, friend, father, mother, child, (or salesperson), doesn't take the time to understand how they truly feel.

Imagine how much easier selling would be if prospects and customers saw you as more down-to-earth, less threatening, and more interested in what they were saying than your competitors. Selling doesn't have to be difficult.

Lesson 13
Voice-mail/Email One-Two Punch

If you are trying to contact a new prospect and you have already left two or three voice-mail messages, but they aren't returning your calls, what should you do? Should you just keep calling and calling, leaving additional voice-mail messages? For most salespeople, this is a familiar scenario, and one that puts them in an awkward position. On one hand, sellers don't want to be pests and bother their customers. On the other hand, they want to be persistent enough to initiate conversation so they won't miss out on an exciting sales opportunity.

I can help you solve this dilemma. Rather than leaving message after message on a prospect's voice-mail system, I have found that it's much more effective to use a voice-mail/email combination to penetrate new prospect opportunities. The progression is simple. If you call a new prospect and they answer the telephone, you have a conversation. But, if the call rolls into their voice-mail system, leave a message—preferably one that piques their curiosity so they will call you back. If the prospect doesn't return your call within a reasonable timeframe, that's when you should switch to email rather than just continue calling and calling.

For example, I might compose a quick email message that says:

Message to: paul.masters@XYZcompany.com
From: tfreese@QBSresearch.com
Date: September 12, 2001
Subject: Quick question...

Hi Paul (or Mr. Masters),

I left a message on your voice-mail system earlier in the week, and while I wanted to follow up, I didn't want to become a pest.

Your counterpart (Doug Trenton) in the Houston office suggested that I touch base with you regarding QBS. Recently, we trained his sales organization on the Question Based Selling methodology and the feedback was "off the charts." Other clients we work with include:

Compaq	Lucent Technologies
Sun Microsystems	Nortel Networks
EMC Corporation	VERITAS Software
3Com Corporation	Clarus Corporation
IBM	Oracle
Merrill Lynch	GE Capital
AOL/Time Warner	...and others

The question is: Would it make sense for us to have a conversation about how Question Based Selling could impact productivity and your sales team's performance? If so, I will be in the office Tuesday and Wednesday of next week. Are you available either of those days for a conference call?

—Tom

If your email message sounds credible, and you are able to pique the prospect's curiosity with a valid reason for making contact, then the initial voice-mail followed by a well-crafted email provides a powerful one-two punch that will get you into many new opportunities that may have otherwise been missed.

Lesson 14
Be Proactive to Avoid Telephone Tag

Suppose you leave a voice-mail message for a new prospect. They return your call, but since you are out, they end up leaving a voice-mail message back for you. You call again, but they don't answer, so you leave another message—and you go back and forth. It's called telephone tag.

Telephone tag is more prevalent today than ever before. In addition to prospects spending more time away from their offices, decision-makers at key accounts use voice-mail to screen their calls in order to limit the number of solicitations they have to deal with. But, when one of these key decision-makers returns your call, telephone tag creates a problem. After going back and forth between voice-mail systems, the prospect's initial curiosity usually gets replaced by an even greater sense of frustration, and their interest in you and your offering will quickly dissipate.

The key is to avoid telephone tag before prospects become frustrated. There are two ways to accomplish this. One is to address the issue head-on when you leave your second voice-mail message. If a prospect has returned your call, and you get their voice-mail system (again) when you call back, you simply say:

Salesperson: "Hi, Mr. Prospect, this is Jane Smith with ABC Manufacturing. I received your voice-mail earlier today. Thanks for calling me back. I was hoping to reach you, but it looks like we're now playing telephone tag. To avoid going back and forth between voice-mail systems, can I make this suggestion? I will be in the office this afternoon until 4:30pm. If you are available today, please call me at (770) 394-0727. If you are not available today, please leave me a message letting me know what time would work best for you tomorrow or Friday, and I will make it a point to be available. I look forward to speaking with you."

Right off the bat, the salesperson here raises the issue of "telephone tag" in an effort to avoid going back and forth. Most people will appreciate your being proactive and respond accordingly. I recommend against leaving voice-mail messages that offer to call the prospect back, however. Your willingness to keep calling and calling can create a sense of eagerness that can easily be mistaken as pushy or overly aggressive.

Email is the other option you can use to avoid telephone tag. After exchanging voice-mail messages with a prospect (first pass), I will often contact them via email with a messaage that says something like, "Mr. Prospect, I received your voice-mail message earlier today. Thanks for returning my call. To avoid playing telephone tag, can we schedule a specific time where we can both be available to get together on the telephone? Perhaps we could even meet for lunch. Would either tomorrow morning or next Tuesday work for you?"

Once again, if the prospect was interested enough to return your call in the first place, being proactive to avoid telephone tag will further increase your credibility in the prospect's eyes.

Lesson 15
Too Available Means, Not Valuable

On a recent Thursday afternoon, I was wrapping up the day's events when the telephone rang. I answered and the person on the other end was a woman who said she represented *Who's Who* in North America. She claimed that I had been nominated for inclusion in next year's *Who's Who* national publication. Instantly, I lit up with excitement. Being selected for a national publication that features important people is quite an honor, don't you think?

This woman from *Who's Who* explained that the next step in their qualification process was a telephone interview with one of their publication editors, who would review my portfolio of personal and professional success.

"Is there any chance you would be available for an interview appointment this coming Monday?" she asked.

"Sure, Monday would be great!" I happily replied.

"What time is best for you?" she probed.

> Eager salespeople often make the mistake of making themselves seem too available.

"What are my choices?" I asked back.

Then, she said something that seemed odd. "Let's see," she said. "Interviews start at 9:00am and last approximately 15 minutes. Right now, we have the following times open: 9:00am, 9:15am, 9:45am, 10:00am and any time from 10:30am to 11:30am." Then she started up with afternoon times, naming virtually every time slot until 5:00pm when the interviews concluded. I couldn't help but wonder how a publication editor's calendar could be so empty. My excitement quickly turned into skepticism. Important people (like editors) aren't this available. As it turned out, my hunch was right. This particular *Who's Who* publication, of which there are many, was just a scam.

There's a lesson here about good communication. How available are you? When an eager salesperson talks with (or leaves a message for) one of their prospects, they often make the mistake of making themselves seem too available. They provide their office telephone number, their cellular number, their pager number, even their home telephone number, in an effort to be more accommodating. Some of the most eager salespeople invite their prospects to call anytime, day or night. The problem is, being too available is more likely to communicate a sense of desperation than credibility.

Salespeople who really *are* valuable are not *always* available. In fact, salespeople who are considered valuable by their customers are usually difficult to reach. That's because they are busy providing important information, new ideas, and valuable solutions to other customers.

To be viewed as a valuable resource, prospects must perceive that you are someone who is in demand. For example, if you tell people that you are available "anytime tomorrow," prospects can easily infer that you don't have anything else to do. Therefore, I would much rather say something like, "I will be in the office tomorrow, although I will be in meetings much of the day. Is there any way we can compare calendars and pick a specific time where we can both be available?" Rather than beg for an appointment, this positioning puts you on par with prospects and customers. It lets them know that your time is important and in demand. As a result, you sound more confident and more valuable.

Along these same lines, I recommend against leaving voice mail messages that say you will be in the office until 5:00pm, especially if you are calling new prospects. Minimum-wage telemarketers work from 8:30am until 5:00pm, not top-notch salespeople. Instead, try concluding your voice mail messages with the following call to action, "Mr. Prospect, if you get a chance, can you please call me back at (770) 394-0727? I will be here in the office until around 4:30pm today (…or before 11:15am tomorrow morning)."

Notice that 4:30pm and 11:15am are both odd times. These odd times tend to generate more action simply because they sound more official, thereby communicating that you have other commitments. Don't get ridiculous on the times though. For example, I would not recommend saying, "I will be in the office today until 10:21am or 4:52pm." These are weird times, and there is a difference between "odd" and "weird."

Lesson 16
Getting One Foot in the Door

Diane Cannady, an enthusiastic but inexperienced salesperson, started selling manufacturing equipment and supplies for a local distributor in Central Michigan. Besides the fact that she was a woman trying to break into a man's world (her words), the company she represented was relatively small and Diane was tasked with breaking into the three largest accounts in the automotive industry: Ford Motor Company, Chrysler, and General Motors.

After numerous attempts to penetrate these accounts, Diane's telephone calls went unanswered. She tried faxing them, but with no better results. Nearing the end of her rope, Diane started thinking "outside the box" in order to come up with an innovative, attention-getting approach that would cause prospects to notice her.

One of Diane's friends worked at a local shoe store that displayed shoes by putting one on the rack, with the mate in the back room. Since they always ended up losing individual shoes, they accumulated a box of orphans that were usually dumped at the end of each month. As a result, Diane was able to obtain an expensive patent leather Italian loafer at no cost. She sent it to one of the key decision-makers at Ford with a note attached that said, *"Now that I have one foot in the door, I wanted to see if…"* Diane included some product information and testimonials from other clients.

Diane succeeded in getting Ford's attention. Not only did she secure an initial appointment, she quickly turned Ford Motor Company into one of her company's largest customers. Sometimes all it takes is a little creativity and a willingness to step outside the box of traditional thinking. As you might guess, there are a lot fewer orphaned shoes in the back rooms of shoe stores in Central Michigan these days.

Lesson 17
Another Way to a Prospect's Heart…

It has been said that one of the best ways to a person's heart is through their stomach. With that in mind, here's another creative idea for penetrating new accounts, one that comes in a pizza box.

Almost everyone loves pizza. Therefore, when direct mail, phone calls, and other approaches fail, one of my more creative clients sends their prospects and support staffs pizza in a box customized with their company's logo and contact information. Along with the pizza, they attach a cordial note that says something like, "We hope you will enjoy a slice of pizza.

We would also like to have the opportunity to earn a slice of your business." According to the Vice President of Sales, the response to this pizza-marketing idea has been excellent and the relative cost for penetrating new accounts is minimal. It just goes to show that a little creativity and extra effort can go a long way toward getting in to see difficult buyers.

Lesson 18
Gain Additional Leverage with Conference Calls

Another way to penetrate new prospect accounts is to leverage your distribution channel of strategic partners, VARs, or resellers. Manufacturers especially, depend on localized providers to recommend their products and services, and then integrate these solutions into the customer's unique business environment.

Leveraging reseller channels is a terrific strategy for broadening sales coverage within a targeted market segment. It gives sellers more "feet on the street" to help identify new prospect opportunities that might otherwise be missed. But sellers must be careful because there is still a need to exercise prudence when chasing leads that come from other channels. In other words, just because you receive a "hot" lead from one of your resellers or VAR partners, doesn't necessarily mean it's worth chasing.

Have you ever been pulled into a deal that hasn't been appropriately qualified? You show up to deliver a product presentation to a large prospect account and none of the key decision-makers are there, just a smattering of nominally influential players. Or, after you wrap up a sales presentation, you discover that the prospect's timeframe for decision is many months (or years) away. Surprises like these are frustrating, to say the least, and you don't need to be wasting your time with them.

> Just because you receive a "hot" lead from one of your resellers or VAR partners, doesn't necessarily mean it is fully qualified.

Let me suggest a strategy that will enable you to avoid some of these problems. When I was in corporate sales, selling technology solutions through various distribution channels, I didn't want to rely solely on reseller partners to qualify accounts. That's why I insisted on starting every sales opportunity with a conference call. If a VAR partner wanted to bring me in for a product presentation, or they needed assistance in closing a sale, that was fine—so long as we started with a three-way conference call between myself, the prospect, and the VAR.

Conference calls are easy to arrange. You simply ask the VAR to schedule a fifteen-minute telephone appointment with the prospect so all three parties can appropriately prepare for the upcoming meeting or event. Any prospect who values your involvement will appreciate the request because you are essentially offering to invest extra effort on their behalf. Of course, if a prospect doesn't agree to schedule a conference call in advance, that should tell you something about the quality of the lead and where you stand in the sale.

This conference calling strategy is more strategic and

sophisticated than just helping to better qualify new accounts, however. It can serve as another catalyst in the sales process. For example, people you meet for the first time tend to be cautious and somewhat reserved, especially when an unfamiliar salesperson is brought into a deal by a value added reseller. The conference call gives you an opportunity to bond with potential buyers in advance to break down these barriers. Now, when you meet the prospect live, because you have already had an opportunity to build rapport, conversations start out with a greater sense of familiarity and they get into more depth.

This conference-calling format also enhances your credibility. Whoever sets up the conference call (i.e. the VAR or reseller) will likely kick the conversation off with some words designed to elevate your value in the eyes of their prospects. Remember, VARs want you to look credible when dealing with their accounts because they want to win the sale too. After the initial introductions, I wait for an opening that signals that it's my turn to speak, and then I will usually jump in and say something like:

Salesperson: "Mr. Prospect, Joe Reseller briefed me on your situation before we got on the telephone today. I should qualify that by saying I don't know everything about your account, but thanks to Joe we don't have to start from scratch.

There are a couple of ways we can handle this call. One option is for me to just talk generically about our solutions. The other option is for us to get more specific and focus on how our solutions would work given the unique-

> nesses of your business environment. Since you're the customer, let me ask: would you rather talk generically, or get specific?"

Prospect: "By all means…let's get specific!"

Salesperson: "Well then, can I ask a few specific questions?"

Prospect: "Sure."

Two points about needs development that were made in my first book have a direct application here. First, it will always be true that, "he who asks the question has control over the conversation." In this case, a few well-placed strategic questions allow me to lead this prospect down a path where we can talk about mutual objectives, thereby fostering a more productive conversation. Secondly, as you will see in Lesson 29, (when we introduce the PAS positioning model), sellers can gain more credibility by asking relevant and intelligent questions than they can by pointing out product features or making claims of superiority. In the example above, when the prospect grants me permission to ask "a few specific questions" (which most will), I am strongly positioned to lead a much more robust discussion about the prospect's needs and the corresponding value of my solutions.

Finally, this conference calling strategy also helps to increase the prospect's sense of urgency for making a decision. Because VAR partners and resellers often sell many different products, they might only be able to give a cursory overview of your solutions, in which case, they only stimulate mediocre interest. When you lead an in-depth and robust conversation on a conference call, you have an opportunity to uncover more needs, identify more reasons for prospects to get excited, and secure a subsequent meeting or presentation.

One more note. No matter how much reconnaissance information you receive from your VAR partners or resellers in advance, you will always have a much clearer picture of an opportunity when you have talked directly with the customer in advance on a three-way conference call.

Lesson 19
Getting More Leads at Industry Trade Shows

A common mistake salespeople make at industry trade shows is leading with their value propositions. Prospective customers come by the booths at a trade show and eager sales representatives barrage them with features and benefits in the hopes of generating leads. But as we discussed earlier, prospects are quick to glaze over when they get deluged with similar-sounding value propositions as they move from booth to booth.

The other mistake that plagues sellers at industry trade shows is trying to qualify opportunities too early. Booth representatives are coached to qualify leads as early as possible. While qualifying new leads is a noble goal, prospects don't respond well when they feel they are being sized-up or have to "qualify" to get your attention.

The best way to maximize your opportunity at industry trade shows is to bond with potential buyers by talking about their problems, not your solutions. You will create more opportunities to engage visitors in your booth by mentioning potential problems than blasting them with the standard barrage of benefits.

> You will create more opportunities to engage visitors in your booth by mentioning potential problems than blasting them with the standard barrage of benefits.

Bonding with prospects on their problems is not a difficult strategy to implement. The key is making sure everyone in your booth is using the same strategy—so when the next prospect who comes into your booth asks, "What does your company do?", you say something like:

Seller: "You know all the paperwork headaches customers are now having to put up with as a result of the new federal legislation? Our product solves this problem, along with several other features that can make your life easier, and your business more efficient."

If the issue being raised is relevant to the prospect, their next question will likely be, "How does your product address this problem?" Of course, their request for additional information gives you the perfect opportunity to engage them in a more in-depth conversation about their needs and your value.

The booth staff at an industry trade show should spend 80-90% of their time talking about the problems their products and services solve and the implications of these problems. Of course, as prospects become more interested in how your solution will address their specific problems, you create opportunities to schedule additional conversations and follow-up events. You must resist the temptation to try and tell prospects everything from the confines of your booth. This would only satisfy their curiosity and eliminate the need to meet with you after the show.

Lesson 20
Reverse Telemarketing

Shortly after I formed QBS Research, Inc., I started receiving tons of sales calls. Registering my company must have triggered something that put my name and contact information on every salesperson's mailing list. As you might imagine, it didn't take long before I got sick of being on the receiving end of so many cold calls. You know, the calls that interrupt an important thought, meeting, or project, where the salesperson is working just as hard to stay on the phone as you are to get rid of them. Trust me, I can get rid of a pesky salesperson with the best of them, but at some point, I would rather just not be bothered.

Since sales training is my chosen profession, it may seem a bit odd that I wouldn't like cold calls, but I don't want to have my time wasted any more than you. This all changed for me, however, on May 7, 1999. That's the day the first shipment of my book, *Secrets of Question Based Selling*, arrived. Suddenly, we had a warehouse filled with books, and thousands of people out in the business world who had never heard of the Question Based Selling methodology. Marketing the book was an integral part of my business plan, and it was definitely time to pull out all the stops.

Later that night, I received a cold call at my house from a fellow named Frank Myers, who represented a mortgage company. My first inclination was to get off the phone as quickly as possible. For some reason, I didn't. Instead, I listened for a few moments and waited for an opening. After Frank's opening blurb, a pregnant pause ensued, so I jumped into the conversation and my selling instincts took over. Here's what happened:

TF: "Frank, can I ask you a question?"

Frank: "Sure, Mr. Freese."

TF: "Since you are in sales, is it safe to assume that you will make a bonus or commission if I buy something?"

Frank: "Yes, we are measured against certain sales goals."

TF: "In that case, do you have access to the Internet?"

Frank: "Yes."

TF: "Do you have a pencil handy?"

Frank: "Yes, sir."

TF: "Good, then write down this website address."

www.QBSresearch.com

I explained to Frank that he should go immediately to this website address and buy the book, *Secrets of Question Based Selling*, because reading that book would do a lot more to increase his income than staying on the telephone with me.

"Thanks for the tip, Mr. Freese." Frank said in an enthusiastic tone, and we politely hung up. Frank felt great because I was cordial and gave him some valuable advice. I felt great because it was suddenly comfortable and easy to get off the telephone.

Later that evening, I checked our website and sure enough, Frank had ordered not just one book, but six—for himself and others on his team. I used the same approach with the next salesperson that called, and they bought books too! Of course, not everyone who called purchase books, but it worked often enough that I discovered a trend. Cold-callers had suddenly become a very lucrative market for QBS book sales. Not surprisingly, receiving cold calls became much less annoying now that we were generating revenue each time we picked up the phone. You might even call it reverse telemarketing.

I realize that this strategy of reverse telemarketing may not apply to everyone's business, but at the very least, if you ever get tired of receiving cold calls from salespeople, do me a favor. Have them call me.

Lesson 21
Better Than Sending Christmas Cards

The first greeting card we receive every holiday season comes from my friend, Mark Reed. As an independent insurance agent,

Mark sends annual holiday wishes to his entire network of customers and friends. But rather than sending Christmas cards, or the politically correct equivalent 'Happy Holiday' cards, Mark sends out 'Happy Thanksgiving' cards. And every year I think, what a terrific idea!

> Most holiday cards are sent out amid the December rush. As a result, they often are received with minimal impact.

Like clockwork, a classy gold or silver foil greeting card arrives at our house the week before Thanksgiving, with a special message of goodwill from Mark and his family for the holiday season. This year, the printed inscription on his card read:

At this season of Thanksgiving,
we wish to express our appreciation for your
friendship and goodwill during the past year.
We wish you a most happy Thanksgiving season!
Mark Reed, CLU

Mark usually includes a short hand-written note with every card to personalize a message for the intended recipient.

Besides meeting the annual obligation of sending holiday cards, this idea of sending Thanksgiving cards is strategically superb. Most holiday cards are sent out amid the December rush. As a result, they often are received with minimal impact. But Mark's Thanksgiving card, because it arrives first every year, gets so much more consideration than regular holiday cards. In fact, when I asked him about it, Mark said that he is always amazed how many customers make a special point of calling and thanking him for the card. How many people make a special point of calling to thank you for Christmas cards?

I also like the congruence that's built into Thanksgiving cards. Being thankful is the point behind the Thanksgiving holiday, which is ultimately the message you want to communicate with holiday cards. Kudos also go to Mark for appreciating his customers' friendship and goodwill and not just their business.

Lesson 22
How to Handle Potential Blockers

One of the questions sellers should always ask when scheduling an appointment or sales presentations is, "Who else needs to be involved?" After all, the last thing you want to hear at the end of your sales pitch is, "Wow, that was the best presentation I've seen in a long time. I only wish my boss, Fred Simpson, had been here to see it." Oops!

But let me give you some words of caution. When sellers ask, "Who else needs to be in this meeting?" prospects are sometimes quick to put up their defenses saying, "I am the only one who needs to be involved at this point." These people are affectionately known to salespeople as blockers.

If you are dealing with the ultimate decision-maker, they alone might be able to make a decision to buy your product or service. If you are selling high-value products or services to large strategic accounts like General Motors, Coca-Cola, or Westinghouse, however, it's unlikely that just one person will make the buying decision. But that doesn't mean they won't try to block you and keep you away from others who will need to be involved in the sale.

Generally speaking, blockers have two motivations for holding salespeople at bay. One is ego—wanting to exert control over the decision process. The other is a directive from their superiors. Every seller wants key executives to be personally involved with their sales efforts, but high level managers cannot afford to involve themselves with every salesperson that calls on the account. Consequently, subordinates are directed to screen vendors and qualify solutions to make best use of the higher level decision-maker's time.

> If you are selling high-value products or services to large strategic accounts it's unlikely that just one person will make the buying decision.

Screening vendors is a legitimate objective, and it is true that you might have to impress a gatekeeper before you get in to see the key decision-maker. That's just part of the game in sales. But when someone blocks you in order to stroke their own ego, their actions can be harmful to your selling efforts. The issue now is how best to respond when you do get blocked.

Ironically, when a blocker's ego is the driving force behind their need to hold you at arm's length, leveraging that same ego is also your best chance for becoming unblocked. For example, when a blocker says, "I'm the only person you need to be dealing with at this point," trying to convince them that they are off-base is a difficult proposition. Instead, I try to change their perspective by asking, "At some point in the future, if you do choose to recommend our product or service, who else will ultimately need to sign-off on your recommendation?" This positioning acknowledges a blocker's importance in the decision. It also causes ego-driven blockers to make your task seem monumental—in which case, they are likely to say:

> **Blocker:** "After you convince me, you will then have to convince the rest of the committee, my boss, the Vice President of Operations, and the executive staff."

Now you have set yourself up perfectly to say, "If all these other people will ultimately have to sign off on your recommendation, would it make sense to invite some of them to next week's meeting, so you don't have to sit through the same presentation four or five different times?"

Having to sit through multiple versions of the same presentation will not sound appealing to someone who is driven by ego. They'll start to recognize that blocking you is a waste of their "valuable time," which increases the likelihood that they will involve other people in the decision process.

Lesson 23
Follow-up with a Creative Questionnaire

Have you ever experienced that awkward time in the prospecting ritual where you are trying to follow-up with a prospective buyer, but they are no longer responding to your voice-mail messages? You're left wondering: Have they lost interest, or are they just busy? Should I be persistent and risk being too pushy, or should I back off and risk missing out on an exciting mutual opportunity? It's a classic Catch-22 scenario.

Don't despair, everyone who sells something will face this dilemma at some point. As for me, I get frustrated when I find myself in limbo, not sure how best to proceed. If there *is* an opportunity to pursue a potential sale, then I would like to engage the prospect further. If not, I would rather direct my selling efforts elsewhere and not become a nuisance.

> You're left wondering: Have they lost interest, or are they just busy?

Several years ago, Greg Cini, a star salesperson with Continental Office Furniture in Columbus, Ohio introduced me to an idea that solves this problem. Essentially, Greg was very creative in developing a questionnaire that he sends out to prospects to break the stalemate. This questionnaire gives prospects an opportunity to respond without feeling pushed. But rather than following up with a boring letter, Greg crafted a humorous but humble, multiple choice response card that elicits a very high response rate from the prospects and customers he is pursuing.

When I tried Greg Cini's idea for myself, I became an instant believer. Now, at QBS Research, Inc., whenever we find ourselves in marketing limbo with a potential client, we send the following questionnaire:

QBS Research, Inc.

Thomas A. Freese
President/Author of:
"Secrets of Question Based Selling"

Sales Training
Motivational Speaking
QBS Methodology Consulting

Mr. Kevin Hazleton
Director of Sales
Fortune 1000 Company, Inc.
Central Park Blvd., Suite 500
Atlanta, GA 30328

Dear Kevin,

I am running out of creative ways to follow-up on our conversation from a couple of weeks ago. As a "sales guy" yourself, it stands to reason that you would appreciate a certain amount of persistence—so I created this simple questionnaire.

Would you please take a moment to check the appropriate box on the response card and return it in the self-addressed stamped envelope?

QBS Sales Executive Questionnaire

(Check One)

____ Yes, we are interested in pursuing Question Based Selling.
Please call me to:
___ Set up Another Meeting
___ Discuss Scheduling Options

____ We are interested in QBS, but don't call until: _____

____ Sales Training is currently:
___ On Hold
___ Under Consideration

____ We have elected not to pursue Question Based Selling
at this time.

____ Leave me alone already!!!

____ Other: _____

Thank you in advance for your time and consideration. Filling in the appropriate blanks and returning this questionnaire will help us both.

Sincerely,

Tom

Especially when I stamp "PRIORITY" on the outside of the envelope, I have found that this technique generates an unusually favorable response. In fact, it's been my experience that most prospects appreciate that you want to be persistent without being pushy. They also appreciate that you are willing to poke fun at yourself by giving them the opportunity to say, "Leave me alone already!" More often than not, prospects who are indeed interested in pursuing a relationship will pick up the telephone and call you directly. Mission accomplished! Thanks, Greg!

Lesson 24
Handling the Literature Brush-Off

Every day, salespeople all over the world are lobbing thousands of telephone calls in to key decision-makers, trying to penetrate new prospect opportunities. If the prospect conveys even the slightest bit of interest, sellers are ready to close for an appointment. Consequently, lots of different salespeople end up asking for a share of the prospect's time and attention.

Prospects are having to be more judicious with their time, however. In today's business environment, there is simply not enough time in a day to meet with every salesperson who calls. As a result, prospective customers are having to be much more discerning about whom they choose to meet. Once in a while, sellers are able to secure a meeting with their first telephone call, but prospects usually hold salespeople at arm's length saying things like, "Why don't you send me some information first? That will give me a chance to review your literature and decide whether or not we should meet."

When one of your prospects asks for literature, do you get excited? Do you think to yourself, "Oh boy, they want information about my solutions!" Of course, you don't. In the real world, most prospects won't ever read the sales literature you send. Sometimes prospects ask for literature because it's the easiest way to get the salesperson off the phone. But be careful. Asking for literature can be a legitimate request. A prospect could be thinking that a little

> Prospects are having to be more judicious with their time.

prudence on their part could spare them from a lot of unnecessary meetings. Either way, if sending brochures doesn't accomplish your objective, let's examine what you can do to handle the literature brush-off.

Old School Defenses No Longer Work

When prospects ask for literature, salespeople are quick to counter with responses like, "What I would rather do is set up a meeting," or, "Would it be all right to bring the literature to you personally?" It's only natural to try and wrangle a face-to-face opportunity instead of just sending literature.

Standard comebacks like these have outlasted their usefulness, however, as they are no longer effective when dealing with literature requests. Why? Because it's likely that prospects who ask you for literature have made this same request to many other previous callers. And it's likely that these other salespeople were also unexcited about sending literature, in which case they probably used similar comebacks and got similar results—they got turned down too.

Granted, some small fraction of prospects, when they hear these standard comebacks, will agree to a meeting. But most will hold their ground since they've already heard similar defenses from countless other salespeople.

What the prospect is really saying is they would rather not meet until they have some evidence that their time will be well spent. Can you see the irony, then, of two sides taking the exact opposite positions? Prospects say, "I don't want to meet until you send information," and the salesperson says, "I don't want to send information until we meet." In today's increasingly competitive business environment, you don't want to be on the other side of this argument.

Changing the Prospect's Perspective

The next time a prospect asks you to send literature, try responding with "I will be happy to send some information to you." Anything other than, "I will be happy to...," will seem like a dodge. But wait. That's not the entire response.

The underlying strategy here is a negotiating position we teach in Question Based Selling called tit-for-tat. The way it works is: when a potential buyer asks you for something, you earn the right to ask them for something in return. In this case, I respond to the prospect's request for literature by saying, "I'd be happy to send you some information. Can I ask you a question first?" Most prospects will instinctively say, "Yes," which positions me to lead the following exchange:

Salesperson: "Should I send a stack of standard marketing literature, or would you rather know more about how our product actually works?

Prospect: "I would rather know how your product works."

Salesperson: "Well, here's the problem. We have all kinds of sales literature and glossy marketing brochures, and I am happy to send them to you. But there is no marketing brochure that explains how our product would impact your specific environment. That's why, for most clients, what we do is get in front of a white board and have a more specific conversation about their needs and our solutions. I would be happy to send brochures, but would it also make sense to schedule a meeting to discuss your specific environment?"

The effectiveness of this strategy is in your ability to change the prospect's perspective. Rather than contradict the prospect directly by coming back and asking for a meeting, my positioning actually changes their request. Originally, the prospect was requesting literature. But when the salesperson in this analogy asked if the prospect would rather have marketing brochures or know how the product would impact their specific environment, of course, most will want to know how the product works. Suddenly, the prospect is asking for something very different than a standard marketing brochure.

If you sell high-value products and services, the reality is you don't have a detailed document that explains exactly how your solution would impact the uniquenesses of the prospect's specific environment. For most salespeople, the solutions you deliver are too varied and complex and are probably tailored to the customer's business. If a prospect is just brushing you off, they won't care what you send; however, those prospects who are truly interested will see the value in meeting with you to discuss your solutions further.

Lesson 25
Practice What You Preach

At the end of the second day of a Two-Day Methodology program for Sun Microsystems, one of the students in my training approached me and asked, "Tom, I really like the QBS methodology and what you teach in your training classes. My question is, what did you *really* do when you were in sales?"

Believe it or not, I get asked this question quite frequently. It was particularly ironic that this person asked, because practicing what I preach is how Question Based Selling got into Sun Microsystems in the first place.

In the fall of 1999, Bruce Ambler, District Manager for Sun's Western Region, asked me to deliver a QBS Methodology training as part of her sales kick-off meeting in Las Vegas. Like any good salesperson, I asked if there were other people outside her group at Sun who would benefit from knowing about Question Based Selling. Bruce suggested I contact John Ryan, the Director of Sun University. I called John several times and ended up leaving a voice-mail message. Then, I followed-up with an email (per Lesson 13).

The Director of Sun University didn't return my calls but he did respond to my email message. He thanked me for my interest in Sun Microsystems and suggested I forward literature about Question Based Selling and the programs we offer. Essentially, his email could be characterized as a standard response to a vendor cold call.

Some sales trainers might get excited when a Director level person invites them to send information about their programs. I mean, Sun Microsystems is a huge company with thousands of salespeople. But, I didn't get excited. While I didn't feel slighted by John Ryan's response, I had to assume that the Director of Sun University is a very busy executive who is constantly being bombarded with sales calls from vendors, all wanting Sun to adopt their respective training programs.

If all I did was forward literature about Question Based Selling, my probability of success would have been statistically slim, similar to what a Sun Microsystems salesperson might experience if they just sent literature out hoping customers would call and order new technology platforms. It just doesn't happen that way. Therefore, while I appreciated Mr. Ryan's invitation, all my sales instincts and my experience were telling me that just forwarding literature to a busy executive like John Ryan wouldn't move me closer to my objective of furthering QBS within Sun Microsystems.

In my reply back to John Ryan, I opened by thanking him for his interest in Question Based Selling. Then I responded to his request for information by saying, "I would be happy to send you information about Question Based Selling and the programs we deliver...except there's one problem. If I just forward the information you requested, I would be doing exactly what I teach sales professionals *NOT* to do!"

Over the next several days, there were a number of private conversations within Sun Microsystems about who this Tom Freese person was, and about his audacity in not sending information to Sun University. In fact, my email response caused such a commotion within Sun that John Ryan himself flew to Las Vegas to attend the Western Regional kickoff and sit though my training. Shortly thereafter, Sun University contracted with QBS Research, Inc. to deliver sales methodology training programs all over the country for Sun's field sales organization. And as they say, the rest is history.

So, to answer the question that this one student and others frequently ask me, let me say, "Yes, Virginia, I do practice what I preach."

Lesson 26
You Don't Have to Apologize for Doing Your Job

There's a big difference between being humble and being subservient. If you help customers by selling valuable products and services, then you shouldn't have to apologize for doing your job. Nonetheless, some salespeople still feel the need to open their conversations by saying, "Mr. Prospect, I am sorry to bother you, but..."

Sellers provide an invaluable service to virtually every industry. Buyers of all kinds depend on salespeople for information, new ideas, solutions, and to help create a longer-term vision as they navigate through their own business challenges. Medical sales reps, for example, provide doctors with information about state-of-the-art diagnostic tools, leading edge procedures, and new medicines. Companies that depend on automation find out about new technologies from salespeople. And, when individuals plan their family's future, they often rely on the expertise of a certified financial planner. Sure, salespeople are getting something in return for their invested effort (i.e. commission dollars or a bonus), but that's fine because sales transactions are supposed to be mutually beneficial. Both parties in the sale should win, and neither party should be subservient.

While it is true that some salespeople are more valuable than others, the mere fact that you are reading this book tells me that you are among those who are committed to excellence. Therefore, you should not have to apologize for striving to provide high levels of value to your prospects and customers.

Lesson 27
Changes in Brochure Etiquette

Companies invest large amounts of money to design snazzy marketing literature that will hopefully grab a prospect's attention and facilitate the sales effort. They use four-color processes with catchy graphics on a heavy, glossy paper stock with the goal being to create an exciting literature package. These companies and marketing staffs are hoping that their professionally crafted brochures will have a significant and lasting impact on the potential buyer.

If you send marketing literature through the mail, first impressions are very important. It is especially critical that the information you send arrives completely intact, without ruffled edges or dog-eared corners especially since you are not there to present it. If you deliver literature in person, however, it's a different story. While the information you present should look pristine when it is first introduced, if it still looks pristine when you leave the meeting, it probably won't have any lasting value for the prospect.

> I always make it a point to write something on my customer leave-behinds.

Sales traditionalists would say that you should write notes on a scratch pad or on the order form, but leave the literature intact. After all, you wouldn't want to mess up your beautiful and expensive marketing literature. I disagree. Snazzy brochures are initially impressive, and customers may flip through some of the pictures and diagrams while meeting with you, but very few actually read marketing brochures in any depth. Consequently, thousands if not millions of sales brochures find the circular file within moments after the sales call ends.

Do you want your treasured literature to end up in the trash? Of course not! Me neither. That's why I always make it a point to write something on my customer leave-behinds. Sometimes I draw on the diagrams to illustrate key points. Other times, I will make notes in the margin about something that's unique to the prospect's environment. I might even write contact information (like reference names) or my cellular phone number. What you choose to write is not even the important part. The key is that prospects are much more likely to save and refer to sales literature that has been personalized in some way for them, rather than saving pristine product brochures that otherwise have little intrinsic value.

Lesson 28
Can You Sell Me This Pen?

Have you ever interviewed for a sales position where the interviewer handed you an inanimate object (like a pen) and asked, "Can you sell me this pen?" I've encountered this a number of times but my first experience would end up having the biggest impact on the rest of my sales career.

With my college graduation date rapidly approaching, I was in a race against time to land a decent job and venture out into the real world. One day, I was running late for my second interview with Xerox Corporation. Wearing a three-piece navy pinstripe suit, I frantically peddled my ten-speed bicycle under the midday sun across the University of Florida campus. I must have been quite a spectacle. I didn't care, as it was an important interview for me. My first meeting with Xerox went well and I was one of several candidates who was asked back to compete for a limited number of sales positions.

With some luck, I arrived at the J. Wayne Reitz Union in good time. This is where most of the student interviews took place. I made a quick stop to get organized and check my hair. I remember looking into the restroom mirror thinking, "I am as ready as I will ever be." Then, I headed off for the actual interview, a little nervous, but also very excited.

One of the Xerox recruiters, John Parkin, came into the waiting area and called my name. It was show time. Mr. Parkin started the interview off with some casual conversation. He seemed relaxed and easy-going. I was trying to remain calm but couldn't help thinking that he was about to ask a series of philosophically intense interview questions. Surprisingly enough, the interview took a different course.

John (he invited me to call him) explained that second interviews with Xerox were structured different than first encounters. He assured me that I had effectively addressed all the "philosophically intense" questions in my first interview. "Frankly, Tom" he said, "your performance in the first interview is why you have been invited back." I felt good about his feedback.

He continued, "Tom, what I would like to do today is spend some time role playing. Would that be all right with you?"

"That would be fine," I said. How could I refuse?

John then placed a very expensive designer pen on the table between us. He explained that role-playing was a common exercise at Xerox. "Let's start with me as the prospect," he said, "and you as the salesperson. Your objective is to sell me this pen. Tom, when you're ready, please begin."

My mind raced...even faster than my ten-speed bicycle. "Sell him this pen?" I thought to myself. "I don't have any experience selling designer pens! Don't people just buy these things off the rack? He already owns the damn pen, for goodness sake!"

Since it was obvious that I should take the ball and run

with it, I picked up the pen and held it between my fingers. I paused for a moment to collect my thoughts, hoping to think of something clever, and then I started the role-play as the pen salesman. Here's what came out:

"Mr. Parkin, this is a fine pen, but it's not just any pen. Let me show you what I mean. This pen is truly a unique writing instrument for many reasons. Some people would even say that owning this pen is a once in a lifetime opportunity.

First, you should notice the fine styling of this pen, black on one end, with embossed highlights on the other. It has a gold clasp for functionality, and the designer look adds prestige, which will distinguish you from other businessmen when the pen is prominently displayed in your shirt pocket or when you pull it out of your briefcase.

This is also a high quality pen; one that will last for years without any problems. Of course, if there is ever a problem, this pen carries a full lifetime warranty. The design also enables its owner to easily replace ink cartridges to give your pen new life—like putting a brand new engine into a classic car." (Good analogy, huh?)

John sat quietly as I rambled on and on about the pen. In fact, the longer he just sat there, the more inclined I felt to fill the silence with benefit statements. As I wrapped up my lengthy diatribe about the pen, I sheepishly asked if he wanted to buy one. He smiled and nodded in a way that signaled to me that he had seen enough. I felt a sinking feeling in my stomach. Something was obviously not right. We shook hands as John thanked me for my time and asked if I had any questions. Then, I left the interview, climbed back on my bicycle, and that was the end of my candidacy for a sales position with the Xerox Corporation.

Heeeeere's Johnny

Late one evening several years later, I was flipping through the television channels when I landed on the Best of Carson—the old Tonight Show re-runs from the mid 70's. Actually, the promotional tickler is what caught my eye, billing Johnny Carson's next guest as the World's Greatest Salesman. I decided to stay up a little bit longer to watch.

After a short commercial break, Johnny came back on and introduced the Greatest Salesperson in the World. I didn't quite understand what criteria had been used to anoint this person with the title of "the Greatest Salesman," but out from behind the curtain came an older man wearing a lemon/lime colored leisure suit (popular at the time—although inexplicably so). I had never heard of this gentleman before, but apparently, this was no spoof.

After exchanging pleasantries, Johnny went right to the heart of the matter. What is it, Mr. So-and-So, that makes you the Greatest Salesperson in the World? Go, Johnny! That was my question as well. Without hesitation, this man claimed that he could sell "anything to anyone."

"You can sell anything to anyone?" Johnny challenged. "Okay, hot-shot," Carson continued, "Let's see if you can sell me something right here on this show." Johnny reached across the desk, picked up an ash tray, placed it in front of the World's Greatest Salesman, and said, "Sell me this ash tray."

Talk about de-ja-vu. Johnny Carson was reenacting the scenario from my college interview with the Xerox Corporation. I couldn't wait to hear how the World's Greatest Salesperson would respond. After all, what can you say to sell an ash tray to a skeptical prospect, with millions of people watching?

Johnny's guest calmly took the ash tray, studied it for a few moments, and then asked, "Johnny, do you ever have a need for one of these on your set?"

"Yes," Carson answered. "Some of our guests like to smoke, so we always have an ash tray on hand for them to use."

"How much would you give me for this one?" the salesman asked.

"I guess a couple of bucks," Johnny replied.

"Sold!"

The audience erupted with applause. He did it. He made the sale! But he didn't sell the ash tray by launching into an endless barrage of features and benefits, he did it using questions—first to identify a need, and then to secure a commitment.

It was clear that I had done just the opposite in my interview experience with Xerox. When I was asked to sell a pen to the Xerox interviewer, I tried to accomplish the objective by highlighting all the different features of the pen and how they would benefit the prospect. It was suddenly clear that a different approach might have produced different results.

What should I have done during the interview role-play? For starters, I should have picked up the pen, held it up to the prospect, and asked questions like:

Salesperson: "Do you currently use this type of product?"

"How familiar are you with this particular model?"

"Would you like to know how this pen could benefit your business?

While interviewing candidates for sales positions, what sales managers really want to know is how a person sells. Do they just spew forth with benefit statements in the hopes that prospects will recognize value, or do they open with questions knowing that in order to communicate value, you must first uncover a need? The real value of this interviewing technique is to find out whether the person you are interviewing is statement-based or question-based. By the way, which type of person are you?

Lesson 29
Re-Engineering the Elevator Pitch

Companies spend millions and millions of dollars to craft the perfect elevator pitch—you know, the introductory value statements salespeople use to kick off their initial sales calls or presentations. What they want is to grab the prospect's attention in order to engage them in a productive dialogue about potential needs and possible solutions. The problem is, with the increasing amount of noise in today's marketplace, beginning a sales call or presentation with the traditional elevator pitch puts a salesperson in an extremely weak position. Let me show you what I mean.

Several months ago, my office assistant received a call from IBM World Headquarters. As it turned out, the Vice President of Eastern Operations for IBM had heard about Question Based Selling from another QBS client, and his administrative assistant was calling to schedule a conference call with me, so her boss could find out more about our training programs.

> Beginning a sales call or presentation with the traditional elevator pitch puts a salesperson in an extremely weak position.

The call was set for the following Tuesday afternoon. I dialed the appropriate number at the prescribed time and was immediately routed into one of those automated conference-calling forums. Honestly, I was a little nervous. As you might imagine, IBM is a lucrative prospect for anyone who delivers sales training. After waiting nervously for several minutes, the VP came onto the conference call, and he was as nice as he could be. He apologized for being a few minutes late and then jumped right into his purpose for calling.

"Tom, I have heard great things about Question Based Selling and the programs you deliver," he said. "We have a new initiative (at IBM) to modify our strategic sales process and based on what I have already heard, Question Based Selling seems like it would help us a great deal. Therefore, Tom, I have blocked off the next 45 minutes on my calendar so you can tell me all about QBS."

Now, let me pause the story right here for a moment. Do

you think this is what someone like myself (a sales trainer) would want to hear from the Vice President of Eastern Operations at a very large prospective client like IBM? The answer is, yes, absolutely! Besides having already heard positive feedback from another QBS client, he was, in essence, giving me a red carpet invitation to tell him all about Question Based Selling.

My head and heart swelled with pride and satisfaction, and the natural tendency would have been to jump in and start "telling" him about the QBS Methodology and all the wonderful things we could do for his sales organization. This is how most salespeople begin their presentations—with some form of elevator pitch.

Don't Forfeit Your Competitive Advantage

The phrase "elevator pitch" is a colloquialism that characterizes the value statements sellers often use to open their conversations with prospective customers. The phrase comes from the scenario that would occur if you suddenly found yourself in an elevator with the key decision-maker at one of your target prospect accounts. Essentially, you would have a small window of time in which to say something that would hopefully be impactful enough to get the prospect's attention. This situation occurs at the beginning of every sales call and product presentation. Knowing that prospects are quick to form impressions, salespeople feel pressure to say something valuable in order to grab and hold the prospect's attention.

Salespeople are not creating these "elevator pitches" on their own. Their companies invest tremendous resources to craft the perfect introductory blurb—an elevator pitch that will give salespeople a magical combination of words that will secure more appointments and maximize the time spent with potential buyers. On the surface, having a good opening line seems to make good sense. The problem is that opening with the traditional elevator pitch is usually counterproductive to the rest of your sales efforts. These introductory blurbs, that sellers hope will differentiate them from other vendors, usually sound just like what everyone else is saying. As a result, their value propositions get instantly commoditized and prospects quickly lose interest, which is exactly the opposite of what we are trying to accomplish at the beginning of our sales conversations.

In the case of my conference call with the IBM Vice President, I could have jumped in with both feet and delivered one heck of an elevator pitch. But I didn't, because I knew that starting with an elevator pitch about Question Based Selling would only forfeit my competitive advantage.

What Impression Do You Want Prospects to Form?

When you first engage new prospects, what percent of them do you think will form an impression of you and your company during the first few moments of your conversation? The answer is 100%. Literally everyone you talk with starts forming their impressions from the very beginning of your conversation. Now the question is, what impression(s) do you want prospects and customers to form about you?

With respect to strategic training programs, I figure most Sales VP's have experienced plenty of sales training over the years. So, it's safe for me to assume that whatever I say about Question Based Selling will be compared to the impressions they have formed from previous training experiences. What I don't want to happen is to have that comparison leave me sounding like the rest of the sales training establishment.

Sure, I could have jumped right into an elevator pitch about Question Based Selling. After all, I am absolutely convinced that the QBS Methodology is very different than traditional sales methods, and I believe anyone who has been through our training would say that QBS provides a highly leveraged sales model that gives salespeople a unique advantage throughout the sales process. But I would like you to hear what my elevator pitch would sound like and then judge for yourself. When you hear it, you might be duly impressed. Maybe you'll even stand up and salute. On the other hand, you might find that my elevator pitch (for QBS) sounds very similar to what every other sales trainer says about their sales training programs. Therefore, I invite you to form your own impression as you read the following introductory blurb. My elevator pitch would sound something like:

Sample Elevator Pitch

"Question Based Selling is a common sense approach to sales based on the theory that what a salesperson asks, and how they ask, is more important than what they could ever say. Therefore, after 17 years in the trenches of corporate sales and management, I developed the QBS Methodology and I now teach salespeople how to penetrate more new accounts, uncover more needs, increase the buyer's sense of urgency, build internal champions, shorten the sales process, increase the size of their sales forecasts, close more deals, increase market share, …blah, …blah, …blah, …blah."

Isn't this what every sales trainer says? It absolutely is! Everyone who offers sales training talks about pipeline generation, penetrating new accounts, handling objections, and closing sales. And you can be sure they all make similar claims of superiority that sales executives have heard many times before. Consequently, when prospects hear the same old pitch, they tend to form the impression that, *"Hey, this person sounds just like everyone else."* Therefore, rather than differentiating yourself, the traditional elevator pitch tends to commoditize your value because you don't sound different than anyone else.

If the company you represent sells high value products or services, you don't want to sound the same as everyone else. Instead, you want to differentiate your solutions, your company, and most importantly, yourself, causing prospects to form the impression that, *"Hey, this person sounds very different and potentially more valuable than everyone else!"*

Bond with Prospects on the Problem

Salespeople who lead with their solutions using the traditional elevator pitch, do so in the hopes of engaging prospective customers in a more in-depth discussion about their needs. After all, uncovering potential problems is what ultimately creates opportunities to make sales. But leading with your solutions, in order to get into a discussion of the customer's needs, follows an illogical progression. Besides the fact that an elevator pitch is so easily commoditized, presenting your solutions first makes no sense. Prospects don't have problems, issues, concerns, or needs because a salesperson happens to call offering a potential solution.

To communicate the value of your product or service, you must first have something to build value against. Therefore, rather than trying to bond with potential customers on your solutions, you will create many more opportunities to provide value if you bond with them on their problems, issues, and concerns. To illustrate this point, let's go back to my conference call with the Vice President of Sales from IBM. If you remember, having heard good things about Question Based Selling, he invited me to tell him about the QBS Methodology. But rather than opening with the traditional elevator pitch and hoping to get him excited about my solutions, I did just the opposite. In fact, here is how my initial conversation with this IBM sales executive actually went.

First, since it's always nice to hear positive feedback from previous client events, I thanked him for his positive comments about my sales training programs. Then I responded to his request for information by saying, "I would be happy to tell you all about Question Based Selling. Can I ask you a question first?"

Of course, he said, "Sure."

With one simple question, I instantly transitioned the conversation out of "presentation mode," and into discovery. This created the perfect opportunity for me to ask questions that would help identify potential needs. Again, practicing what I teach, I started with a series of diagnostic questions—a QBS technique that allows the seller to establish credibility early in the dialogue.

> **TF:** "How many people are currently in your sales organization?"

VP: "Approximately 330."

TF: "Does that include Systems Engineers?"

VP: "No," he said, "that's another 110 SE's."

TF: "Do you currently leverage an inside sales organization?"

VP: "Actually, two," he said. "One of our inside sales teams is in the Northeast, and the other is in Atlanta."

TF: "Are most of your people centralized in regional sales offices or spread out in a virtual office environment?"

VP: "We have several regional offices, but many of our sales-people are transitioning to a virtual environment."

Once I kicked the conversation off with a series of relevant and intelligent diagnostic questions about his business environment (See *Secrets of Question Based Selling,* Chapter 8), I switched gears with my questions to focus on needs development, and bonding with prospects on the problem. Let's continue the dialogue.

TF: "Well, let me ask you this. Do you have salespeople out in the field trying to penetrate new accounts, making lots of sales calls and leaving lots of voice-mail messages, but not being called back?"

VP: "We absolutely do!" he said. "Penetrating accounts at a strategic level is a big challenge for us."

TF: "Question Based Selling will solve that!" I said.

VP: "How?" he asked.

TF: "I'll get to that in just a minute," I said. "While we're talking about challenges, let me ask you about something else. Do you find that with newly hired salespeople, some ramp up in a very short period of time while others struggle along and sometimes never make it over the hump?"

VP: "Yes. Ramping new salespeople up is another challenge."

TF: "QBS solves that too."

VP: "How?" he asked again.

Suddenly, the conversation we were having was very different than it would have been had I opened with the standard elevator pitch. Let me say it again. You bond with prospects by focusing on their problems, not on your solutions. Take my example as a case in point. After raising some key business challenges, you earn the right to engage decision-makers (like this VP) in a productive conversation about their needs and your solutions. Bonding with prospects on their problems is also the key to broadening the sale by creating many opportunities for you to provide value. Let me show you what I mean.

Expand Your Opportunity to Provide Value

If the products and services you sell offer numerous benefits, then you'll want to give qualified buyers multiple reasons to buy from you. That's why it's important to broaden the scope of your sales conversations to include a variety of different areas where your products and services can add value. Remember that we want to bond with prospects on their problems, but we also want to increase their sense of urgency by expanding their needs and giving them many reasons to move forward with a purchase. Expanding their needs will also expand your value proposition, which will increase your probability of success in making the sale.

What problems do *your* prospects and customers face? In technology sales, for example, customers consistently encounter business issues like reliability, manageability, and upgradability in their daily routines. If you sell manufacturing equipment, issues

> You bond with prospects by focusing on their problems, not on your solutions.

like inventory, cost containment, or time-to-market might be areas of concern for potential customers. If you sell financial services, then business issues like timely reporting, margin requirements, or the institution's track record, might be in the forefront of your customer's mind.

Whether you sell medical supplies, telecommunication services, consulting, or durable goods, you can easily build a list of key business issues that typically drives decisions in those selling environments. But let me share an observation that may shock you. Key business issues like reliability, manageability, upgradability, inventory, cost containment, time-to-market, reporting, margin requirements, and a company's previous track record usually aren't the driving force behind strategic decisions. While issues like these are often the focus of the typical elevator pitch, they usually don't cause people to make buying decisions. Instead, the implications of the business problem, and the corresponding benefits of your solution drive most buying decisions. What do we mean by implications? The implications of a problem are the underlying hot buttons that cause problems to be important to your specific customer.

Suppose You Were Selling Water Pumps

To show you how implications can expand your opportunity to provide value, here's a simple exercise I use when delivering "live" QBS training programs. For the next few minutes, let's suppose you work for a company that manufactures and sells a product that's very different than your daily routine. Let's pretend you are in the business of selling water pumps. Your target market is homeowners who have flooding problems in their basement, and your company offers a solution that can pump the water out. Note: For the skeptics who are thinking, "I don't understand how an example about selling water pumps will help me," I invite you to buckle your seat belt, as this exercise may radically change the way you interact with prospects and customers in the future.

Back to our example, let's suppose that you receive a lead and tomorrow, the two of us (you and I) are going to call on a new prospect who has a flooded basement. Before we actually go on this sales call, however, let's spend a few minutes strategizing together about how we want this call to go. We would want to be on the same page when we get in front of the customer, and strategizing in advance will give us an opportunity to "arm" ourselves with a broader list of implications that will enable us to expand the prospect's needs and increase their sense of urgency for making a decision.

The first step in our strategy session would be to identify the customer's problem. Given the scenario I just described, it's relatively obvious what the prospect's problem is—they have water in their basement. Seems simple, doesn't it? Be careful, though. Many sellers, upon hearing about a problem in their sales calls, jump immediately into their value propositions, saying, "Hey, let me tell you about my pump!" But guess what? People don't buy water pumps because they have water in the basement. They buy water pumps because of the potential implications that could arise as the result of having a flooded basement.

To strategize about potential implications, let's ask the question: Why might water in the basement be a problem for this customer? While there is no way to know a customer's specific hot buttons before we actually meet with them, we can absolutely prepare ourselves in advance of the call by identifying potential implications we think might affect their decision. Therefore, if we worked together to create a top-ten list of potential risks that homeowners face as a result of having flooded basements, we would end up with a list of implications that includes the following:

Water in the basement *could*...
   ...cause structural damage to the home.
   ...damage personal property.
   ...create a mildew or odor issue.
   ...present certain health or safety risks.
   ...affect other systems in the house (AC, electrical, etc.).
   ...create a huge inconvenience.
   ...lead to an insurance hassle.

…increase stress within the household.

…reduce the homeowner's property value.

…end up costing lots of money.

This list of implications represents the driving force behind every water pump purchase. Think about it this way. If a prospective buyer isn't concerned about things like structural damage, property damage, health risks, odor issues, their time, stress, insurance, and cost, then you probably won't sell them a water pump. But, to the extent you can lead the conversation toward these potential implications, you can significantly expand the prospect's sense of urgency by giving them multiple different reasons to buy from you.

Two Common Mistakes

To put this concept in perspective, we must jump out of our hypothetical strategy session and fast-forward to tomorrow's sales call—to think about what might actually happen when we meet the prospect face to face.

Knock-knock-knock. When the homeowner answers the door, we introduce ourselves by saying "Hi, my name is Tom Freese and this is my assistant, (insert your name) and we're from XYZ Water Pump Company. How can we help you?"

The prospect responds saying. "I've got a flooded basement."

This is where the traditional salesperson, upon hearing a problem, has an intense urge to jump into their value proposition, saying, "Let me tell you about my pump!" Of course, the value proposition at this point in the sale would take the form of an elevator pitch where the prospect hears something that sounds like…blah…blah…blah. But as I said earlier, starting off with the traditional elevator pitch puts you in a weak position because your value proposition gets instantly commoditized. Furthermore, if you want prospects to have more than one reason to buy from you, then you will want to uncover multiple implications of the problem, thereby providing you with multiple opportunities to build value. In other words, when a prospect says, "I've got a flooding problem in the basement," we want to steer the conversation into a more in-depth discovery of what their specific hot buttons are.

Be careful with your questions, however. Just because you want to uncover a prospect's hot buttons doesn't mean they want to be probed. For example, if a prospect says, "I've got a flooded basement," an inexperienced salesperson might be tempted to try and uncover implications by asking, "Why is flooding in your basement a problem?"

What do you think happens to a salesperson's credibility when a prospect wonders why they are being asked such an obviously rhetorical question? Most prospects would wonder, "Huh?" Prospects are always forming their impressions, and asking valueless questions will only compromise your credibility. Asking overly rhetorical questions is one of two common mistakes that can cost you an opportunity. To avoid this scenario, I use a simple technique that ensures a more robust conversation. Let's revisit the scenario.

Knock, knock, knock. Door opens.

Salesperson: "Hi! My name is Tom Freese and this is my assistant (insert your name) and we're from XYZ Water Pump Company. How can we help you?"

Prospect: "Thanks for coming. We've got a flooded basement."

Salesperson: "Besides the obvious, getting rid of the water, can I ask, what are you most concerned about?"

A non-rhetorical question like this one will invariably cause prospects to start naming specific implications, like concerns about structural damage, damage to personal property, or potential health risks. That's because probing beyond the obvious encourages potential buyers to think in terms of the specific hot buttons that are causing them the greatest concern.

This concept applies to virtually every value-driven sale. When I was in technology sales, it was fashionable to run around talking about issues like downtime, growth, system manageability, and support. But these issues rarely justify a purchase by themselves. Instead, it's the implications of downtime, growth, system manageability, and support that increase the prospect's sense of urgency and cause them to move forward with a decision. That's why I always look for opportunities to ask questions like: *"When your computer system goes down, besides the obvious issue of getting the system back on-line, what are your biggest concerns?"* Questions like this cause prospects to focus on the implications of computer downtime, which gives you an opportunity to uncover the customer's specific hot buttons, like how system outages cost their company an estimated $10,000 per hour, or how, without the computer, they are unable to properly service their customers. Once again, the problem of system downtime by itself creates a whole series of potential implications related to the system being unavailable. This logic applies whether you sell technology, medical supplies, financial services, or manufacturing equipment.

What are the chances that a water pump prospect will rattle off a list of ten or twelve implications that mirror the list we created in our strategy meeting? The answer is slim to none. Most prospects will only name one or two, or every once in a while, three implications.

This brings us to another common mistake sellers make when probing for needs. We sellers have been conditioned to assume that it's our job to uncover needs. And of course, we want to uncover multiple implications so we will have many opportunities to provide value. Too often, though, sellers keep probing and probing until the prospect cuts them off, saying, "Please don't ask me any more questions! Just tell me what your product does!" Getting cut off by a prospect and being prematurely thrust into your presentation of benefits puts a salesperson in a weak position.

Pushing harder and harder to draw more implications out of your prospects will only cause them to turn against you. Furthermore, we as sellers shouldn't assume that it's our job to get prospects to state their own needs. In fact, here's a secret for you. Raising potential implications with your prospects and customers creates one of the greatest opportunities for salespeople to establish credibility early in the sales process.

Raising Implications Increases Your Credibility

Preparing a mental list of potential implications in advance puts you in a strong position to have more productive sales conversations. Rather than probing to try and get prospects to state their own needs, you can significantly increase your own credibility by bringing up potential implications in the conversation. Let me show you what I mean using our previous example.

To guide the conversation toward potential implications, earlier we suggested that you ask, "Besides the obvious, getting the water out of your basement, what are you most concerned about?" Suppose the prospect names two implications by saying that he is concerned about two things, *cost* and *structural damage*. Rather than jumping directly into your sales pitch, you have a wonderful opportunity to bring up additional implications by asking, "What about *personal property*? Do you have any furniture or personal items in the basement that could be damaged by the water?"

If the implication you raise is relevant to the prospect's situation, as in this case, you are likely to hear, "Yes, we do have some antiques and keepsakes stored in the basement that we would like to protect." Bingo! You have just uncovered another opportunity to add value. You have also earned the right to probe for additional implications.

Using this technique, you can create all kinds of opportunities to add value by asking implication questions like:

Salesperson: "Is the flooding problem affecting any other systems in the house like a downstairs furnace, water heater, air conditioner, or electrical circuits?"

"Are you starting to sense any odor or mildew issues?"

"What about safety concerns? Do you have any small children?"

Guess what happens to your credibility every time you bring a relevant implication up to a qualified prospect? You guessed it. Your credibility goes up. Way up! The reason is simple. You bond with prospects on their respective problems, not on your elevator pitch. And the more successful you are in expanding their problems (via implications), the more opportunities you will have to add value.

Something else happens when you bond with prospects on their problems. In my first book, *Secrets of Question Based Selling*, I made the point that salespeople start the sales process with near-zero credibility. It's still true. Buyers today are skeptical. But, when they form the impression that *"Hey, this salesperson might be able to help me,"* they start helping you, help them.

> When prospective customers form the impression that you might be able to help them, they lower their defenses and start helping you, help them.

For salespeople, this is a huge point! Therefore, I will say it again. When prospective customers form the impression that you might be able to help them, they lower their defenses and start helping you, help them—to solve their problems. Herein lies the difference between potential buyers who are cautious and standoffish, holding salespeople at arm's length, and those who choose to engage in mutually beneficial business relationships. You simply cannot succeed in making a sale until a customer helps you to help them. That's why we're doing this, to create a strategy where more prospects will want to engage in more productive conversation.

Position Away Your Competition

Bonding with prospects on their problems creates opportunities for salespeople to offer potential solutions. And, at this point, it's natural for sellers to jump ahead into their respective sales presentations. But jumping ahead in the sales process usually isn't the most productive approach.

Ironically, the most productive way to position the value of your product or service begins with a discussion of possible alternatives, and why they might not offer the best solution. This is a very different approach than most salespeople take. Most sellers take an SPA approach to the sales process. They open with a series of introductory statements that focus mostly on their solution (S), usually in the form of an elevator pitch, hoping to gravitate into a more in-depth discussion of the prospect's problems (P). Later on in the conversation, the focus will naturally shift to a discussion about how their solutions compare to the other alternatives (A) that are being considered.

We already talked about the fallacy of starting off with the traditional elevator pitch. When it comes to positioning potential alternatives, there are similar challenges. Most sellers tend to be reactive when it comes to discussing their competition. They avoid the issue until customers start asking comparative questions. Avoiding these comparisons forfeits a wonderful opportunity to add value, however. One way to add value in a sales conversation is helping customers identify needs. We discussed how you can accomplish this earlier by bonding with prospects on their respective problems (P) and implications. But, we can also add value when it comes to positioning our solutions against possible alternatives. Doesn't it make sense to help potential customers think through their decision alternatives in order to help them realize that your solution is the best?

That's why I favor the approach of proactively raising potential alternatives, in order to position them away as *not* the most effective. To succeed in making a sale, prospects must conclude that because they have problems (P), that won't be addressed as effectively by other competing alternatives (A), they would be better off choosing your solution (S). In Question Based Selling, this is our PAS positioning model, which is much different and more effective than traditional SPA selling methods.

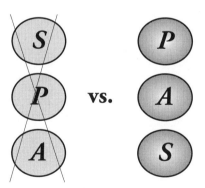

Think about it this way. Your value proposition is strongest after you have successfully positioned away other competing alternatives as not offering the best solution. Successfully positioning away other competing alternatives naturally opens the door for you to provide greater value. How does this work in real life? Let me show you by going back to my conference call with the Vice President of Sales from IBM. If you remember, I opened the dialogue by asking a series of short-answer diagnostic questions to establish credibility and kick off the discovery process. Next, I bonded with him on his problems (P) by asking:

> **Your value proposition is strongest after you have successfully positioned away other competing alternatives as not offering the best solution.**

TF: "Do you have salespeople out in the field trying to penetrate new accounts, picking up the telephone, leaving lots of voice-mail messages and not being called back?"

VP: "We sure do."

TF: "What about new hires? Do some people ramp up in a relatively short timeframe, while others struggle along and sometimes never make it over the hump?"

VP: "Yes (again)."

TF: "QBS solves that, too."

I could have jumped right into a presentation of the QBS Methodology, but I didn't because I first wanted to differentiate Question Based Selling from other sales training alternatives (A). You will see this next as we pick up the conversation.

TF: "As you know, Mr. Vice President of Sales, there are a couple of ways to do sales training. One approach is to hire a sales enthusiast, someone who will come in and tell funny stories in order to get your sales organization excited. The problem is, if salespeople return to their desks and gravitate back to their old approaches, they will get the same results—in which case, hype tends to wear off relatively quickly.

Another approach to sales training is to implement a methodology that requires salespeople to fill out massive spreadsheets that document every nuance in their accounts. The problem with this approach is, giving a salesperson a blank spreadsheet, doesn't guarantee prospects and customers will want to share that much information.

That's why at Question Based Selling, we take a common sense approach that will differentiate your salespeople from the rest of the masses."

Did you hear the (A)? If you noticed, I didn't engage in mud slinging. I didn't ever refer to my competitors by name. That's because talking someone else down only makes you sound defensive. The technique is called *subtly poisoning.* Essentially, the strategy is to gently (but proactively) poison other alternatives in the prospect's mind, in order to position them away as *not* offering the best solution.

Critics of PAS might argue that it's better just to focus on your solutions and wait for prospects to bring up potential alternatives. I disagree for two reasons. First, what if the prospect waits until the end of the conversation (or sales presentation) to ask how your solution compares with other potential alternatives? Do you really want to spend the last few minutes of your sales call or presentation talking with them about not buying from you? Second, since most of your prospects are going to consider various alternatives anyway (other than buying from you), I would argue that if you don't help them compare your proposed solution to other alternatives, your competitors will.

Positioning away your competitors is not a complex process. When prospects consider alternatives (other than yours), they basically have three options. They could choose to do nothing, thereby maintaining the status quo. Frankly, the decision to do nothing is often one of your toughest competitors. Another option is for prospects to try and solve their problems by themselves. Lastly, they can choose to purchase a competitive product or service from someone else. With a proactive effort on your part, any of these alternatives can be positioned away early in the sale, thus clearing the way for you to differentiate your solution and more effective in addressing their needs.

Going back to our water pump analogy, if you were talking to a prospect with a flooded basement, after you succeeded in bonding with them on the problem, you could subtly poison the alternative of doing nothing (for example) by saying something like: "Mr. Prospect, one option you have is to do nothing, and put off your decision until later. The problem is, issues like potential structural damage, mildew, and safety risks usually don't go away by themselves. If anything, they tend to get worse and increase the extent of the problem."

If you were selling computer software, and found yourself in a meeting where key decision-makers of a Fortune 500 company were considering the option of installing your software themselves, you could subtly poison this alternative by saying: "Mr. Prospect, you certainly have the option to install this software on your own. The challenge is that most of the customers we work with already have more responsibility than they can handle. As a result, they're trying to make their to-do lists shorter, not longer. Frankly, that's why they partner with us, to leverage our expertise with this software, so they can focus on other important projects."

When customers are considering proposals from other vendors, you can position these alternatives away using the same techniques I used in my conversation with the VP of Sales for IBM. In either case, the objective is the same. We want prospects to recognize that their problems (P) are not going to be addressed as effectively by other alternatives (A), therefore, they would be much better off by choosing our proposed solution (S).

Be Ready to Present Your Solutions

As I have said many times before, salespeople cannot offer any value, to any customer, at any time, ever, until that customer recognizes the existence of a need. Whose job is it to uncover needs? It's the salesperson's job. Once you have covered the prospect's needs, and have positioned other alternatives away as not the most effective, you are then in a strong position to communicate the benefits of your proposed solution.

So, what benefits does your solution offer? Oddly enough, the answer to this question may not be as obvious as you think.

Companies spend millions of dollars trying to craft a value message that will differentiate their products and services. The sales organization is then pumped full of benefits to take these value messages out into their respective territories. If we take a closer look at these benefits, however, we might discover that what a salesperson thinks is valuable, and what a prospect thinks, are quite different.

To illustrate, I am going to take you back to the water pump analogy one more time. Remember when we were strategizing in advance of the call? Well, after we developed the need and thought about how to position away other alternatives, it would be time to strategize about benefits. Therefore, let's take a moment now to do just that, by asking ourselves, "What are the benefits our proposed water pump offers?"

The natural tendency for many sellers is to point out benefits such as speed, the fact that the product is quiet, and its excellent service record after the sale. The problem is, these aren't benefits to the buyer. Your solution may be fast, quiet, and serviceable, but that's not why people buy water pumps. People buy water pumps because of the implications of having a flooded basement. Remember? Implications like structural damage, damage to personal property, potential health risks, mildew, odor issues, and the resulting monetary expense, are ultimately what cause potential buyers to move forward with a water pump purchase.

What does this mean for salespeople? It simply means that the real value you offer should be a reflection of the implications that get uncovered during the discovery stage of your sales conversations.

In one of the examples we referred to earlier, computer downtime was the problem. For salespeople, it's tempting to hear prospects talk about issues like downtime and want to immediately jump into a benefits presentation. But if you take the time to drill down and identify different implications of the problem, you can create multiple opportunities to build value. Examples of implications caused by system downtime include reduced revenue, customer dissatisfaction, time-to-market issues, end-user complaints, and a negative reputation in the marketplace. Implications like these are the true buying motivations behind every purchase. Therefore, salespeople must recognize that the real benefits they offer should be a reflection of these implications, as they are ultimately what drives purchase decisions.

> The real value you offer should be a reflection of the implications that get uncovered during the discovery stage of your sales conversations.

There is a hidden advantage here for salespeople who want to differentiate themselves and their solutions. Virtually every business issue can be broken down into multiple implications—at least ten, as we discussed earlier. Just ask yourself, "Why might this (issue) be important to the customer?" For those who are analytically inclined, this has a mathematical significance. Identifying multiple implications for every issue gives sellers exponentially more opportunities to add value, and it also gives prospects more reasons to buy from you. When we talk about closing strategies later in the book, uncovering more needs will also help support your prospect's efforts to cost-justify a favorable decision for your product or service. Everybody wins!

Summary Point

To make a long story short, the message here is don't start your sales conversations with the traditional elevator pitch! This is a point I emphatically make when speaking to sales audiences all over the world. I am not against talking about your solutions. I just believe that in today's increasingly competitive marketplace, the traditional SPA approach commoditizes your value proposition with "generic sounding" claims of greatness. Instead, using a PAS model and bonding with prospects on their problems, puts you in a much stronger position to uncover more needs and communicate greater value.

Lesson 30
Beware of the Question, "Why?"

When someone makes a comment or asks a question, we often want to know what's behind their question or comment. So, we ask, "Why did you say that?" …or, "Why do you ask?"

Do people like it when you are interested in what they are saying? The answer is a resounding yes! We can make the argument, therefore, that asking "why" is a way to show that you are interested in what someone else is saying. But that's not always how the question "why" gets interpreted.

Rather than show interest, the question "why" often puts people on the defensive, especially when they feel you are challenging their argument or their intelligence by asking your question. The risk is that prospects and customers will misinterpret the intent of your question by thinking you are being critical or judgmental. Of course, when people feel that they are being judged, they put up their defenses. Marriage counselors deal with this every day—one spouse asks a simple question that balloons into a full-fledged argument, all because he or she asked "why," or "why not," and the other felt threatened, jeopardized, or attacked.

The problem comes from the fact that the interpretation of the question "why" is oftentimes different than the asker's intent. Here's an example of how your intent could easily be misinterpreted in a sales conversation. In an attempt to uncover potential needs, a salesperson who wants to know what caused a prospect to choose their current vendor might ask, "Why are you using XYZ Company as your current supplier?"

The prospect, on the other hand, who is interpreting the salesperson's intent, might hear, "Why in the world would you want to do business with such a shabby outfit?" If a prospect feels you are challenging their previous decision, it's no wonder they would get defensive.

The remedy for this is relatively simple. To reduce your risk of putting others on the defensive, replace the question "why" with the question "what." This puts you in a position of lower risk where you can make the same inquiry by asking, "Mr. Prospect, what caused you to select ABC Company as your current supplier?" The use of the question "what" here has a neutralizing effect that's more likely to produce a mutually productive response.

Lesson 31
Don't Be a Talking Head

Sales engineers and other sales staff personnel often get dragged into sales calls and presentations only to have the salesperson turn to the audience and introduce them, saying, "Gary is our product expert and he's going to tell you about all our wonderful solutions. So, go ahead, Gary, tell them."

Gary has just been introduced as a talking head. Without regard to the prospect's unique circumstances or environment, Gary is essentially being asked to spew forth with goodness in the hopes that prospects will recognize value. Even if Gary was briefed in advance, it's difficult to create a sense of mutual value without first establishing the customer's needs as the backdrop for the presentation. At the very least, putting someone in the position of a talking head creates an awkward moment in the meeting.

I am not picking on sales support people. The same thing happens to salespeople when your internal champion introduces you to their boss saying, "Cindy, tell him what you told me about your extended warranty!" Suddenly, Cindy is thrust into the talking head role to spew information about her company's extended warranty. But, as we already emphasized, telling is not selling, and the idea of spewing forth with goodness only forfeits your opportunity to add value against the prospect's specific hot buttons.

Like many of you, I've always wanted to control my own destiny, especially in sales. The talking head role feels awkward because it puts sellers in a position of weakness in the conversation. Fortunately, for you, me, and the rest of your sales team, it's relatively easy to regain control of your destiny.

Transition from "Telling" Into Discovery

The next time you are thrust into the talking head role, here's a simple technique that will put you back in a position of strength, so you can provide maximum value. To illustrate, let's go back to the scenario where the salesperson introduces his sales support person as the product expert saying, "Gary is going to tell you about all our wonderful solutions. So, go ahead, Gary, tell them."

While it would be natural to jump directly into "tell mode," and start rattling off a barrage of generic-sounding features and benefits, Gary has a unique opportunity to regain control of the meeting and establish his credibility in the process. All Gary has to say is, "I would be happy to tell you about our solutions. Can I ask a couple specific questions about your business environment first?" Virtually everyone will say, "Sure." Bingo!

Gary isn't dodging the issue, and he's not shirking his duties to provide valuable information. In fact, he is being very forthright and direct in agreeing to tell the customer about his company's solutions. But, by using this simple technique, Gary can easily transition the conversation out of presentation mode and into discovery.

This transition is important because in the PAS positioning model we explained earlier, buyers don't have needs because their salesperson happens to be offering a valuable solution. Instead, the opposite is true. The only way a salesperson can provide valuable solutions is to establish needs to build value against. By asking a few questions before jumping into his presentation, Gary gains an opportunity to build credibility and uncover needs that will ultimately fuel the prospect's interest in the solutions he is prepared to discuss.

After transitioning the conversation into discovery mode, what questions should Gary ask? Some salespeople would be tempted to ask detail-oriented, gut-wrenching probative questions in order to uncover the prospect's pain. I don't recommend this. Many prospects aren't ready to share their pain this early in the discovery process. Instead, the technique we teach salespeople in Question Based Selling is to open with a series of short-answer questions that probe the status of the opportunity. Asking relevant and intelligent questions gives you an opportunity to establish your credibility. Prospects are always forming their impressions. Therefore, if you ask a series of relevant diagnostic questions, prospects will automatically perceive higher levels of competence, credibility, and value.

> The only way a salesperson can provide valuable solutions is to establish needs to build value against.

In the example, after Gary gained the prospect's permission to ask a couple "specific questions about their business environment," he could have very easily asked status questions like:

Q: How many end-users do you currently support?
Q: In how many different locations?
Q: Are these locations centrally or remotely managed?
Q: How fast is your service business growing?
Q: How many technicians do you currently have on staff?

If the diagnostic questions you ask are relevant to the prospect's environment, they will see you as a knowledgeable resource and they will also appreciate that you have done your homework. Once you have established your credibility, you can easily transition the conversation back into presentation mode by asking, "How familiar are you with our different solutions?"

Very few people will claim absolute knowledge. Most will say that they have some familiarity, but will then leave the door open to be educated further. This enables you to ask, "Would it be valuable for me to take a few minutes and bring you up to speed on our family of products?" This puts you in the perfect position to educate them on the value of your solutions as they relate to their specific needs, which is very different than being thrust into the role of a talking head.

Lesson 32
Develop World Class Listening Skills

There are two kinds of people in this world—those who are always striving to learn more about themselves and others and those who are content with what they already know. Which type of person are you? Most of us would like to be the type of person who is open to learning new things and genuinely interested in other people. But in selling, this is oftentimes the exception rather than the rule.

Over the years, salespeople have been conditioned that it's our job to communicate the value of our products and services. Therefore, we show up and want to "tell" prospects all about our solutions. In fact, the old school of selling has always held the belief that being more emphatic when positioning benefits increases your probability of making the sale. There is a fundamental flaw with this thinking, however. To assume that prospects and customers are always open-minded and ready to hear whatever a salesperson has to say is a mistake. It's more likely that being overly emphatic will cause prospects and customers to feel pushed, in which case, they will probably push back, which makes the traditional approach of communicating value an even greater challenge.

When you show interest in other people, those people will tend to show greater amounts of interest in you.

Once again, the problem is, telling is not selling. While it's important for sellers to establish credibility in order to build relationships, too often we attempt to gain credibility by "telling" how much we know. We try to impress prospects by using fancy buzzwords, name dropping, or sharing self-indulging stories. But if you notice, potential buyers are usually not impressed. It's more likely that they will retreat or clam up, not wanting to be around someone who thinks he or she already knows everything.

You see this at many social gatherings. Have you noticed that there is always someone at the party who goes on and on telling about themselves? After boasting about their latest vacation, they brag about how smart their kids are or how well their investments are faring on Wall Street. But if you look closely, you will see that these people who spend most of their energy telling about themselves usually have trouble maintaining an audience. That's because people don't want to hear all about you. Instead, they want you to be interested in them.

The secret to being a good communicator is simple. When you show interest in other people, those people will tend to show greater amounts of interest in you. This premise serves as the foundation for every successful relationship...in sales, in social situations, in business, and in your daily personal life. So, let me ask you: What are you doing to show other people that you are genuinely interested in learning more about them?

Passive Listening vs. Active Listening

The first listening skills class I have ever attended was in 1987. My sales manager at the time thought the entire sales organization would benefit from a half-day seminar designed to instill good listening skills. I was skeptical. What's a listening skill? Are they going to teach us how to cock our heads to one side, like the RCA dog, to improve our hearing abilities?

Sure enough, my first listening skills experience turned out to be a valuable one, and I still use many of the concepts I learned on a daily basis. The most impactful thing I took away from this class was the realization that there are two different kinds of listening—passive listening and active listening.

Passive listening is the physical act of hearing. This is what husbands do. Sorry, guys, to let the cat out of the bag, but the phrase, "Yes, dear," really means, "whatever you just said isn't very important to me." Not surprisingly, passive listening does not do much to further the conversation or build better relationships. In sales, one of the most common examples of passive listening occurs when a salesperson is busy thinking of their next question while the customer is still answering their last one. How could you be paying attention to what the customer is saying if you are thinking about something else?

Active listening is something completely different. Rather than just hearing the words, active listening is the act of participating in what's actually being said. How can you actively participate in what someone else is saying? Simple—by being interested enough in what they are trying to communicate to take the conversation deeper. Of course, the best way to further a conversation is by asking good questions. Isn't that strange? One of the most effective listening skills one can have is the ability to ask good follow-up questions about what someone else is saying.

There are several different types of follow-up questions you can use to further your conversations with prospects and customers. I don't want to duplicate my first book, *Secrets of Question Based Selling* here, but I do want to emphasize a few key questioning techniques that we teach salespeople to help improve their listening skills.

1.) *Ask Follow-up Questions.* Do people like it when someone is genuinely interested in what they are saying? Absolutely! Asking follow-up questions is one of the best ways to communicate this interest. If someone mentions that they are pursuing a new business venture, for example, you can very easily increase the depth of your conversation by asking questions about the current business climate, office space, or timeframes for ramping up the new business.

2.) *Can I Ask You a Question?* Before I start probing for needs, I almost always ask prospects, "Can I ask you a question?"

If it's an appropriate time in the conversation, they almost always respond by saying, "Sure." Now, I have been invited to probe more deeply which tends to create a more receptive audience.

This phraseology is also valuable when you want to change the subject in your conversations. When the topic being discussed begins to exhaust itself, you can easily move onto something fresh by saying, "Can I ask you a question about (insert new topic)?" Do people like it when you are interested in their opinion? Yes, again!

3.) *Clarify Vague-O-Nyms.* Perhaps you remember learning about synonyms, homonyms, and antonyms in high school. Synonyms are words that have similar meanings—like big and large. Homonyms are words that sound the same, but have different meanings—like hair and hare, or sense and cents. Antonyms are opposites—like tall and short. So, what's a vague-o-nym? A vague-o-nym is a QBS term we use to define words or phrases that are too vague to have a discernible meaning without additional information.

For example, someone might say, "We are getting ready to sell our commercial property in Chicago." In this sentence, what does the phrase "getting ready" mean? *Getting ready* could mean they are going to take action in the next few weeks. It could also have a longer term context and mean within the next year or so.

The English language is highly imperfect and often quite vague. Oddly enough, this vagueness can be beneficial to your sales efforts by giving you an opportunity to demonstrate excellent listening skills. Clarifying vague-o-nyms, when they arise in your conversations, is a valuable listening skill. Once again, people want you to be interested in what they are saying.

4.) *Ask Global Questions.* A global question is another QBS term we use to characterize questions that further the conversation. Global questions are communication vehicles we use to say, "Tell me more." But rather than commanding someone to tell you more, it's more productive to simply ask global questions like, *How do you mean? ...And then what happened?* Or, *...How will this affect you in the future?*

Global questions are powerful tools for finding out where you stand in the sales process. Essentially, they encourage people to share information with you about the status of the sale. Global questions are also great listening tools as they demonstrate that you are genuinely interested in what other people are saying.

Ask Questions to Provide Maximum Value

When someone asks a question and we know the answer, the natural tendency is to jump right in and answer the question. After all, it makes us feel good and valuable when we know the answer to questions that get asked. The problem is, providing cursory information with off-the-cuff answers usually forfeits an opportunity to provide maximum value.

A prospective client may ask a stockbroker, "What do you think are the best investments in today's market?" Someone who is familiar with the market might be tempted to rattle off his or her favorite investment vehicles. Again, being able to answer the question makes us feel smart. But, it also puts the salesperson in a position of weakness. Wouldn't the best investment depend on the investor's current financial status and their tolerance for risk? Doesn't the best investment also depend on the condition of the different markets? To provide valuable advice, the stockbroker in this example needs more information. And with a few simple questions, he can identify a client's specific needs, which is much more valuable than just responding to their generic question.

This is something you can practice in your everyday life. I do. When my wife Laura comes to me, for example, and says, "Would you like to volunteer for a project at the school?" before answering the question, I first ask, "What project?" To me, there is a huge difference between signing up for a six-month project and volunteering for an afternoon activity.

In my business, I also use questions to qualify training opportunities. When a client calls and asks if I am available the week of October 23rd, before answering, I would ask, "What's happening during the week of October 23rd?" I am not trying to dodge the question. I just would like to know what the customer is asking for before making a commitment that I can't keep. As you can imagine, there is a big difference between being available for a conference call and traveling across the country for a three-day sales training program.

Summary Point

How you have communicated with people in the past is much less important than how you will choose to communicate with them in the future. Therefore, as I said in the preface, given that prospects and customers will be sharing their thoughts, feelings, and concerns with somebody, that *somebody* might as well be you. I believe that how you choose to communicate with people has a lot to do with achieving this result.

Lesson 33
Listen for the Question Behind the Question

We just talked about how important it is to listen intently to the questions your prospects and customers ask. It's equally important to understand what they are *really* asking for, and why. Too often, salespeople hear a question and then jump in to respond to what they thought was being asked, only to discover later that some other motivation was actually driving the question.

Perhaps you've heard the story about the young father who was relaxing in the backyard hammock when his ten year-old daughter approached him and asked, "Daddy, what is sex?" Fumbling for a response, the father looked into the innocent eyes of his little girl and decided that it was time to tell her the facts of life. Although he had always assumed this would be her mother's job, the dad hoisted his daughter into the hammock and began to explain the differences between boys and girls and where babies come from.

The daughter listened intently as her father concluded his explanation. "Thank you, daddy," she said, getting down from the hammock.

Curious, the father turned to her and asked, "What made you want to know about sex?"

"Gym class," she replied. "On the parent permission slip, I didn't understand the box that reads…Sex: M or F."

The father in this story answered the question that was asked. And he did a fine job at that. What he didn't do, however, was take the time to understand *why* the question was being asked.

Very few questions are so well articulated that they cannot be expanded or clarified to uncover the person's true motivation in asking. Once again, as a salesperson, you must ask yourself, do you want to provide average value or maximum value? If you want to provide maximum value, then you must listen for and understand the question that's actually being asked. You might even say, the question behind the question.

> Very few questions are so well articulated that they cannot be expanded or clarified to uncover the person's true motivation in asking.

Suppose, in another example, that someone from out-of-town were to ask you, "What is the best way to get the airport from here?" It might seem logical that the best way to respond would be to simply give them directions from here to the airport. But be careful. Isn't it true that the "best" way to the airport, because of traffic patterns and rush hour, might depend on their time of departure? Might the "best" way to the airport also depend on whether they are renting a car or taking public transportation? Wouldn't the "best" way to the airport also depend on how familiar they were with the area? Giving complex directions to someone who is already lost would only confuse them further. If you take the time to listen carefully for the question behind the question, you might discover that the question this person is really asking is, "How should I go to the airport…given that my flight leaves at 7:15pm, I have to return a rental car, and I'm not very familiar with the area?" Responding to the more specific question puts you in a much stronger position to provide maximum value.

What Customers Really Want When They Ask For References

To cite another example of the importance of listening for the question behind the question, let's examine what happens when a prospective customer asks for references. Particularly in larger sales, customers ask for references. They want a list of people they can call to exercise due diligence and verify the benefits of your proposed solution. This request usually sounds something like, "Can you provide some references, people we can call who are already using your product or service?"

Many salespeople, upon hearing this request, respond by providing a list of happy customers. They go back to their respective offices, call around to find out which customers are most satisfied that day, and they put together a well-groomed list of glowing references. Mission accomplished.

There is a problem inherent with this approach, however. If a prospect asks you for references, it's likely that they will also ask your competitors for references too—in which case, your competitors will all scurry back to their respective offices and prepare a similar list of happy customers. As a result, prospects end up receiving a reference list from every vendor, all filled with names of happy customers.

But, have you ever noticed that while prospects usually ask for references, they often never bother to contact them?

Why do they do that? Asking for customer references is certainly a legitimate request, but for the buyer, receiving a bunch of similar-looking reference lists doesn't necessarily help them distinguish between competing vendors. Frankly, they aren't just looking for a list of happy customers. What they really want is to reduce their risk of making a bad decision. Therefore, when a prospective buyer asks for references, what they are really asking is, "Can you please help reduce my risk of making the wrong decision?" If a salesperson understands the

> Have you ever noticed that while prospects usually ask for references, they often never bother to contact them?

customer's motivation in asking the question, they will be in a much stronger position to differentiate themselves and their solutions.

Lesson 34
The Irony of Reference Selling

In my first book, I made the point that traditional reference selling is highly overrated. And as we just discussed, providing a list of happy customer references makes you sound just like everyone else. Virtually everyone you compete with can provide a similarly glowing list of "happy" customers—in which case, you don't succeed in differentiating yourself, and the prospect isn't any closer to discerning which vendor offers the best solution.

Frankly, providing a list of "happy" customer references misses the larger point. As we pointed out in Lesson 33, the reason prospects ask for references is to reduce their risk of making a bad decision. Potential buyers want to know that you have satisfied customers, but they also want to uncover any potential pitfalls or hidden problems that could arise, before making a commitment to purchase your product or service.

> The reason prospects ask for references is to reduce their risk of making a bad decision.

Kevin Kirksey, Vice President of Sales at Centigram, introduced me to his unique strategy for delivering references that is very effective. Rather than providing a standard list of happy customers, Kevin responds to these requests by saying, "Mr. Prospect, I could give you a list of references, just like everyone else. It might be more helpful, however, for you to talk with some of our customers who have had problems, so you will know how we respond when faced with a challenge." Then, Kevin proceeds to provide a handful of customer references who have experienced some kind of problem with their purchase or implementation.

On the surface, this strategy may see a bit odd. But Kevin has found that customers who have had problems that the sales team was able to resolve make terrific references. It's worth noting that virtually every customer on your reference list has had some sort of problem or challenge with the purchase or implementation of your product, so your reference list doesn't even have to change, just the way your references are being positioned.

It's a credibility play. Customers in today's market are smart enough to realize that there are no perfect vendors or solutions. What they really want to know is how you are going to deal with problems when and if they arise.

Lesson 35
One Smart Son-of-a-Bitch

Speaking of credibility, *eCompany Now magazine* recently published an article featuring Naveen Jain, Chairman and Founder of a very successful wireless web company called InfoSpace. Initially, my curiosity was piqued by the title of the article, which read,

Naveen Jain is the Absolutely, No-Doubt-About-It, Einstein-Was-a-Chump, Look-Ma-No-Calculator, One-Zillion-on-the-SAT, Greatest High-Tech Entrepreneur of All Human History (And if you don't believe it, just ask him.)

The article explained that, as a very astute surveyor of the technology landscape, Mr. Jain is able to win people over by the sheer force of his personality and in-depth intellect. "Simply sell yourself (to the customer) as one smart son-of-a-bitch," Naveen Jain says, "and whatever you are selling will sell itself." How's that for a no-fuss, no frills sales strategy?

Lesson 36
The Flip Side of Confidence

The flip side of confidence is humility. While it is important to feel powerful and self-assured, it is sometimes more productive to take a softer, more humble approach. If you allow me to step back in time a few years, I'll show you what I mean.

Mary Frances Gilreath was ninety-five years old when she passed away in November 1998. She was my wife's grandmother. We called her Granny. I had the pleasure of knowing Granny for the last twelve years of her life, and by all accounts, she was a marvelous woman who left behind several legacies, not the least of which were her famous dinner rolls.

At holidays and special occasions, whenever the family would come together for a meal, Granny always apologized profusely for her homemade dinner rolls. "These rolls are overcooked,...or, too dry,...or, they just didn't turn out right," she would lament. Of course, everyone within earshot would immediately come to her rescue, reassuring her saying, "What are you talking about, Granny, these rolls are the best you have ever made!"

I now find that the same principle occurs in business. As an example, the next time you deliver a proposal, if you position the document as a perfectly packaged, fully comprehensive work of art, most prospects will immediately start looking for problems. They will scan your work looking for mistakes, omissions, and other discrepancies. If, on the other hand, you applied Granny's approach and inserted a little humility into your presentation, you might get better results. "Although this proposal contains lots of information, I still wish I had had more time to make it look better," you might say. In response, you will be surprised at how quickly prospects will rescue you saying, "No, no, the proposal looks fine. Thanks for your help in putting it together on such short notice."

If we take this idea one step further, we find that while most people shy away from their weaknesses or mistakes, in an odd way, acknowledging your weakness puts you in a unique position of strength. Let me show you what I mean with an every-day example.

> Acknowledging your weakness puts you in a unique position of strength.

Suppose you were walking through the double glass entrance doors of a large office building when a strong gust of wind blew and caused the doors to slam in the face of the person behind you. It would be easy to say, "That wasn't my fault, the wind did it," placing the blame on the gust of wind. But, you would still feel bad, and the other person may still give you a wicked stare. If, on the other hand, you immediately said to the other person, "Oh, I am so sorry. I should have held the door with two hands. Are you all right?", you would instantly feel better, and in all likelihood, the other person would come to your rescue saying, "Yes, I'm fine. Thank you."

You've heard the adage: "An apple a day keeps the doctor away." This saying is referring to one's physical heath. If, however, you want to improve your emotional health, or just boost your outlook on life, the formula is just as simple: spend less time justifying your actions and more time acknowledging your weaknesses. In addition to making yourself feel better, others will appreciate your humility, and you will be surprised at how fast they come to your rescue.

So, Granny, thank you for the tip!

Lesson 37
The Greatest Salesperson Ever

Recently, I was on a conference call talking with the Vice President of Sales for a large manufacturing company about the possibility of putting his sales organization through QBS methodology training. Essentially, these conference calls are like interviews, where the client wants to make sure that the trainer/speaker's message is robust enough for their intended audience. I completely understand the need to interview sales trainers ahead of time. Frankly, it's how most of my relationships with new clients begin.

This interview became particularly interesting when the Vice President of Sales threw me a zinger, which instantly transitioned the conversation from course content, into a discussion of personal philosophy. "Tom," he asked, "who in your opinion is the greatest salesperson ever?"

This might have been a great interview question, but for me, it posed a certain philosophical dilemma. Should I choose myself and claim that I am the greatest salesperson, in order to convey a sense of confidence that would hopefully put me in good stead? Or, should I take a more humble approach, cast my ballot for someone else, and be judged by the quality of the person I selected? I knew instantly that this question was trouble.

The greatest salesperson ever? Fortunately, my instincts took over, and I responded with the first thought that popped into my head. "The greatest salesperson ever would have to be Mrs. Bill Gates. By tying the knot with her husband, the founder of Microsoft and the richest man on the planet, Mrs. Gates increased her net worth by billions of dollars. Although I consider myself a pretty good salesperson, that's more than I ever earned by closing a single deal."

After the Vice President of Sales stopped laughing, we went on to schedule my first engagement with what is now one of my largest and most successful clients.

Lesson 38
Cut Your Customers a Little Slack

After an initial conversation with a prospective customer, or a sales presentation, some sellers always make it a point to take the lead in following up with their customers. I know plenty of them—salespeople who work hard to think of legitimate reasons to call customers again and again. While there's nothing wrong with staying in touch with your prospects and customers, it might be smart to devote some time to thinking of ways you can get customers to call you back. In other words, if you are always offering to follow up with your customers, they will never feel a need to follow up with you.

In sales, it is important to demonstrate that you are interested in earning the customer's business. But there is a fine line between showing interest and being a pest. Some sellers, for example, send a fax to a prospect and then immediately follow up by calling and asking, "Did you receive my fax?" Others send brochures out through the mail and then call customers to ask, "Did you have a chance to review the literature I sent?" Customers can easily feel pushed by this.

If you are always offering to follow up with your customers, they will never feel a need to follow up with you.

I would much rather put the ball in the customer's court to follow up with me. That's why, on the cover sheets of the faxes I send to customers, and in my email messages, I jot a quick note saying, "Please call me after you've had a chance to review this fax. I will be in the office today until 3:30pm."

Granted, there is some risk that customers may not be as responsive as you would like in calling you back. Then, their lack of responsiveness should tell you something about where you actually stand in the sale. On the flip side, when customers are very responsive, you have more reason to believe that you are looking good in the account. Simply put, you won't find out how responsive your prospects and customers are toward you unless you are willing to cut them a little slack and let them take the lead in following up with you.

Lesson 39
Arm Yourself with More Ammunition

The effectiveness of any sales methodology largely depends on its implementation. If you agree with my analysis that the traditional elevator pitch puts sellers in a weak position by commoditizing their messages, then the next step is to strengthen your position in targeted accounts by increasing the size and scope of your value proposition. The greater your value proposition, the easier it is to motivate potential customers to make buying decisions.

> The easiest way to increase your prospect's sense of urgency is to give them multiple reasons to buy from you.

It's a logical progression. One of the keys to closing more sales is increasing your prospect's sense of urgency for making a decision. The easiest way to increase your prospect's sense of urgency is to give them multiple reasons to buy from you (i.e. multiple benefits). To have an opportunity to position multiple benefits, however, you will want to increase the scope of the opportunity by uncovering multiple needs (i.e. implications). This was the crux of Lesson 29 where we introduced the PAS positioning model.

In one of our earlier examples, we concluded that people don't buy water pumps because they have water in the basement. Rather, they buy water pumps because of the implications of having water in the basement. For example, standing water could cause structural damage to the foundation of the home, destroy personal property, pose heath or safety risks, create odor or mildew problems, cost money, increase stress, and reduce the property value of the home. These implications (of having water in the basement) become the driving forces behind the prospect's buying decision.

Identifying multiple implications with prospects and customers gives you as the salesperson an opportunity to make the problem bigger. Of course, this expands your opportunity to position multiple benefits. It also increases the prospect's sense of urgency by giving them multiple reasons to buy from you, thus increasing your value proposition and making it easier to cost-justify a purchase decision.

Too often, companies rely on their marketing departments to create a list of benefits and then disseminate this information out to the field as ammunition for salespeople to use with potential customers. The trouble is, benefits that get crafted in the ivory tower at corporate headquarters are not always significant differentiators in the field. In technology sales, for example, corporate technology giants like Cisco, Hewlett-Packard, Oracle, Nortel Networks, Lucent Technologies, Compaq, Sun Microsystems, IBM, and Microsoft are all out there saying similar things. If you talk with their salespeople or read their sales literature, it's uncanny how these different technology companies all have very similar value propositions—touting benefits like Scalability, Availability, Manageability, Performance, Productivity, Cost-Effectiveness, Support Services, and Company Leadership. While these benefits may sound impressive, if your value proposition sounds just like everyone else's, you will forfeit your sales organization's competitive edge.

When I was selling in the technology field, I didn't want to sound the same as my competitors. I wanted to differentiate my value proposition and myself, to increase my probability of success in making a sale. I accomplished this by arming myself with more ammunition and focusing on the implications of an issue, not just the issue itself.

I didn't talk with prospective customers about scalability. Instead, I talked with them about the implications of scalability, and how growth would impact their business in the future. Of course, the implications of growth include such things as increasing the number of end-users, adding new software applications, increasing the volume of data, adding locations, adding web services, upgrading technology, dealing with time-to-market issues, cost-effectiveness, ongoing support, and customer retention. (That's ten!) While my competitors spent most of their time talking about scalability, I expanded my opportunity to provide value by getting prospects to think about all the different implications of scalability. If you do the math, you see that I suddenly had ten opportunities to provide value instead of only one. Using this same technique, I identified ten or more implications for the other technology issues we addressed including Availability, Manageability, Performance, and Productivity. This enabled me to expand the scope of my needs-development conversations with prospects, and exponentially increase the size of my value proposition.

Here's a simple exercise you can do to expand your value proposition. On a notepad, make a list of the business issues your prospects and customers face. Be sure to make a robust and complete list. Then, for each business issue on the list, ask yourself, "What are the potential implications of this issue?" In other words, besides the obvious, why might these issues be important to your customer? Push yourself to create a list of ten or more implications for each business issue. The resulting list of implications will arm you with ammunition that can then be used to expand your opportunity to communicate value and increase the prospect's sense of urgency for making a decision.

I recently delivered QBS Methodology Training for Lucent Technologies; and during the program, we split the audience up into small work groups for this same exercise. The objective was to arm Lucent's sales organization by creating a repository of potential implications that prospects and customers were encountering on a daily basis. Each sub-group was assigned two specific business issues, and their job was to construct a list of potential implications. After finishing the exercise, we broke for lunch.

When I returned from lunch early to prepare for the afternoon session, one of the attendees, Danny Shannon, was in the presentation room working on his laptop. Danny Shannon is a perennial top performer at Lucent. In fact, he is the type of guy who radiates success the instant you meet him. Since Danny seemed busy, I quietly went about my business. After a few minutes, however, I noticed that Danny kept moving from table to table in the training room.

"Danny, can I ask why you keep moving from table to table?" I said.

"I'm inputting the implications for all of the different business issues that were created by the various work groups in this morning's exercise," he replied. He was literally going from table to table collecting implications and creating his own person repository of business issues and their resulting implications. Needless to say, I was duly impressed.

When the program resumed, I opened the afternoon session by sharing my observations about how Danny had spent his lunch break. I philosophized to the group saying that there were only two possible explanations for Danny wanting to capture this information. Either his success at Lucent has caused Danny to focus on his sales approach, or Danny's desire to focus on strategy (in this case, arming himself with a comprehensive list of implications in order to expand his value proposition), has caused Danny to become extremely successful at Lucent. I think it's the latter.

Lesson 40
Winners Help Customers Write the RFP

Have you noticed that by the time a request for proposal (RFP) is sent out by a prospect account, the sale is pretty much over? Before the RFP goes out, the customer has developed criteria that will likely determine who will win the business. Even so, the ritual ensues where competing vendors invest countless hours and dollars preparing proposal responses that they hope will win the business. In nine out of ten opportunities, however, the vendor who actually wins the sale is the one who helped write the RFP.

Request for proposals are compilations of the criteria that will be used to make a buying decision. It stands to reason, therefore, that sellers have a much better chance of winning when the criteria being used for the decision closely matches their solution. But who is responsible for establishing the criteria for the evaluation and decision? If you leave it up to your prospects to establish their own criteria, the RFP may not reflect your areas of strength, or it could be so generic as to invite more competition. Worse yet, if you don't help prospects define the criteria for their decisions, your competitors will.

> In nine out of ten opportunities, the vendor who actually wins the sale is the one who helped write the RFP.

The key to working with prospective customers to craft the criteria for their decisions is getting involved early. Sellers today tend to spend lots of time explaining their products and services, but with today's high pressure, run and gun mentality, they spend relatively little time on the front end working with prospects to develop criteria that will bias the decision in their favor.

If one of your competitive advantages is a link to the Internet, for example, then it is essential that you help prospects understand that having a link to the Internet is important—so they will make an Internet link a requirement in their selection process. If another advantage you offer is a long-term warranty, you would once again want customers to include a long-term warranty as a requirement for the decision. You can use this same technique to downplay any competitive weaknesses you may have. For example, if a competitor's product offers more safety features, you would position your product as extremely safe, and then work to convince the customer (in advance) that any additional safety features would be overkill and an unnecessary expense.

Let me put it like this: if somebody is going to help the customer develop criteria for their decision, that person might as well be you. This will increase your probability of success in making a sale. But you must be proactive. It's much easier to build your solution's capabilities into a prospect's RFP than to try and bolt them on as additional features later in the sale.

Lesson 41
Avoid Selling the Cadillac

When I sold high-end Superservers for NetFrame, our partners and resellers often referred to our flagship product as the Cadillac of servers. Usually, this was an attempt by our partner's to pay our product the ultimate compliment. They wanted customers to view NetFrame's family of products as the highest in quality, performance, and value.

Thanks, but no thanks. While it may seem a little odd, I didn't want people to think of NetFrame as the "Cadillac" of servers. Even if they meant it as a compliment, prospective buyers usually don't choose the most luxurious, top-of-the-line product. For example, do you have a night-light in your home? Is it the absolute best, top-of-the-line night-light? No, I bet it's one of the small, inexpensive ones you can buy at Wal-Mart or the grocery store. That's what we have too. Why don't people have the most expensive and luxurious night-lights? Because it's difficult to justify paying a higher price for a product that has equivalent function and serves the same basic purpose as a cheaper one. I had the same problem with NetFrame being labeled as the Cadillac of servers.

Ask yourself this question: What's the difference between a Cadillac and a Ford Taurus? Frankly, these two automobiles are functionally equivalent. Both have combustion engines, glove compartments, gas tanks, windshield wipers, headlights, and they both can seat up to five adults comfortably. Of course, the Cadillac is much nicer and more luxurious. But for a customer whose primary interest is functionality, it might be difficult to justify paying a premium price for a product or service just because it's "more luxurious."

While I appreciated the intended compliment, I did not want prospects to misinterpret my product's position in the marketplace. I especially did not want customers to view the NetFrame superserver product as "functionally equivalent" to what other competitors were offering. Very few customers would have been willing to pay $100,000 (or more) for a superserver that provided the same basic function as a $25,000 PC server, just because it was nicer.

Since the NetFrame product could consolidate up to eight PC servers onto a single platform, it was indeed functionally superior. Therefore, I altered the marketing analogy. Instead of building a comparison between two sedans, I explained to customers that the capacity of a PC server might be analogous to that of a station wagon, where the NetFrame superserver was the functional equivalent of an eighteen-wheeler. This comparison more accurately communicated our ability to provide significantly more capability, and it enabled me to give customers a better depiction of the difference between our product offering and other alternatives.

Lesson 42
Everyone is in Sales

It's not unusual to hear sales trainers or sales managers make the point that everyone is in sales. I couldn't agree more. Virtually everyone who touches the sales process can influence customers and impact the outcome of a sale, either positively or negatively.

In my early days as a sales trainer, I used to make this point, especially when my audience was mixed with salespeople, sales support, sales managers, marketing professionals, and customer service people. But I began to notice that the phrase, "Everyone is in sales," was not being well received. Salespeople showed a negative reaction. They were thinking, "Wait a minute, everyone else can't do what I do." Sales support professionals would think to themselves, "What do you mean I'm in sales? I'm the one who actually understands the product." Sales managers were thinking, "I used to be in sales, but I have since been promoted." Marketing people were thinking, "We're not sales. Our job is to identify target markets and set product direction." And, since the service organization inherits all the customer problems left behind by salespeople, they weren't quick to accept pride-of-ownership in the sale either.

While most people agree with the underlying concept once it's explained, communicating the message that everyone is in sales has proven to be somewhat of a challenge. That's why I decided to switch gears. Now, when I want to make the point that lots of different people can affect the sale, I focus on the functional aspects of each person's role in the sales process. For example, if you think about a salesperson's daily routine, the sales function essentially breaks down into four distinct areas: Communication, Education, Problem Solving, and Customer Service. With the exception of expense reporting, everything a salesperson does all day, every day, falls under one of these four categories.

The question is, what do you do all day, every day? In my view, the answer is the same. Whether your title is sales, sales support, marketing, management, or customer service, your job function still breaks down into the same four disciplines. Everything you do all day, every day, falls under the heading of either communication, education, solving problems, or servicing the customer. For that matter, if you were a high school principal, a lawyer, an accountant, or a hospital administrator, the bulk of your day would be spent communicating, educating, solving problems, and serving the needs of your customers. Therefore, I will let you decide: Isn't everyone in sales?

Lesson 43
The Oldest Rivalry in Business

I have worked with thousands of consultants over the course of my professional sales career, and it's amazing how many of them don't like to think of themselves as "salespeople." Some consultants even view the role sales plays in business as a necessary evil. Salespeople, on the other hand, especially the ones who have ever had to pull an all-nighter to respond to a 1,000+ page RFP authored by a big-eight consulting firm, tend to view consultants as just plain evil.

Seeing as how this book was written by a salesperson (yours truly), I thought it would be fun to share a little anecdote about consultants that recently came to me on the Internet. Maybe this will help to even the score.

Once upon a time, a shepherd was looking after his sheep on the edge of a deserted road. Suddenly, a brand new Lexus Sport Utility vehicle screeches to a halt next to him.

The driver, a young man dressed in a Brioni suit, Cerrutti shoes, Ray-Ban glasses, and a Yves Saint Laurent tie gets out and asks the shepherd, "If I guess how many sheep are in your flock, will you give me one of them?"

The shepherd looks at the young man, then looks at his sheep grazing, and says, "All right."

The young man connects his notebook to his global cellular, logs into a NASA GPS positioning system, scans the ground, opens a data base filled with algorithms, and prints a 150-page report on his high-tech mini-printer. Then he turns to the shepherd and says, "You have exactly 1,586 sheep here."

"That's absolutely correct," the shepherd says. "You can have your sheep." So, the young man takes a sheep and puts it in the back of his Lexus SUV.

The shepherd then turns to the young man and asks, "If I guess your profession, will you return that sheep to me?"

The young man answers: "Yes, why not."

The shepherd says, "You are an Andersen consultant!"

"How did you know?" asks the surprised young man.

"Very simple," answers the shepherd. "First, you showed up without being called. Second, you charge me to tell me something that I already know. Third, you do not understand anything about what I do, because you just took my dog!"

Lesson 44
Internal Champions are the Real Salespersons

How much sales training have you been through in your career? This is a question I often ask when speaking to "live" sales audiences. If you have been selling for some time, then you have probably been through plenty of different sales training courses. This creates an interesting irony, because even with all the training, you may not even be the actual salesperson in your accounts.

Particularly if you are dealing with large corporate accounts, decisions that affect multiple areas of the business tend to involve multiple people. And most of the larger purchasing decisions are generally made behind closed doors; in which case, if you are the designated salesperson handling the account, you probably won't be present when the vendor-of-choice is selected, or when the actual purchase decision gets made. That means, to win the deal, someone in that meeting must be willing to explain why your proposed solution is better than other alternatives being considered. This person who goes to bat for you in the account is your internal champion, and they are the real "salesperson" in your accounts.

When purchase decisions involve multiple players, the salesperson on the account usually doesn't have the time, energy, or opportunity to build personal relationships with every person who will ultimately have a voice in the final decision. That's why it is so important to build internal champions who can convey your value proposition and secure the buy-in of other key players.

Building champions is one of the keys to success in selling. As I wrote in my first book, *Secrets of Question Based Selling*, "A champion who understands how to sell your product or service is worth their weight in commission checks." Your internal champions should be viewed as the real salespersons in the account because they are the ones who must ultimately convince the boss or the rest of the decision committee to support your proposal. They must favorably position the value of your offering, and they must deal with any objections that are raised. When you win a sale, it's usually because the champions in your account were able to articulate the value of your product or service. When you lose a sale, many times it's because your internal champion wasn't strong enough to carry your company's flag in a convincing manner.

It's likely that you have had some professional training thus far in your sales career. But how much sales training have your internal champions had in their careers? I bet the answer is very little. If your internal champions were professionally trained in sales, they would probably be pursuing a career very similar to yours. So what happens is, champions rely on whatever practical experience they have accumulated over time, and most salespeople spend very little time thinking about what they can do to enhance their internal champion's selling skills.

To me, this presents a unique opportunity. The sheer recognition that you are not the only salesperson in the account can give you a distinct advantage over your competitors. And what you do to make your champions better salespeople will go a long way toward differentiating you and your solutions from the rest of the masses.

> If you don't invest the time to make your internal champions better stewards of your value proposition, your competitors will.

Everything I teach, in my books and in "live" sales training programs, is one hundred percent transferable to other people. In effect, you can use the skills and techniques I teach to improve your own sales effectiveness, or you can use them to raise the effectiveness of your entire sales team. Who is on *your* sales team? Sales support people. Managers. Customer service personnel. Consultants. Partners. And your internal champions. Put it this way. If you don't invest the time to make your internal champions better stewards of your value proposition, your competitors will. Let me give you an added bonus. Loading champions up with positioning ideas and working with them to fine tune their value messages will raise their confidence when positioning your solutions, which will in turn, increase your probability of success in making the sale.

Everybody talks about benefits, but only a few salespeople ever take the time to teach their internal champions how to more effectively articulate their value propositions to other key people within the account.

Lesson 45
Can I Ask a Favor?

I don't mean to challenge anyone's theology here, but the assertion in the Bible that says, "Ask and ye shall receive," isn't necessarily true. Just because you ask for something doesn't mean the other person will automatically give it to you. Sometimes it depends how you ask.

The primary role of a salesperson is to facilitate the sales process. In this role, salespeople are constantly asking for things. We ask customers for their time, and then we ask them for commitments in order to move the sales process forward. We also have to sell internally when we ask the appropriate resources from management or corporate headquarters to assist us in closing a sale. As you might guess, salespeople who are most effective at making these requests usually are the ones who end up having their wishes granted.

> When you are sincere in your requests, humble, and respectful of the other person's right to say "No," it's amazing how quickly other people will jump in to help you.

The days of being aggressive and demanding are over. Have you ever noticed that the more demanding someone is, the less they actually get accomplished? Fortunately, the opposite is also true. When you are sincere in your requests, humble, and respectful of the other person's right to say "No," it's amazing how quickly other people will jump in to help you.

Most people will help you if they are motivated to. With

that in mind, here's a magic phrase that you can use to soften your requests and make them more productive. Ready? The next time you want something—a favor from a systems engineer, a faxed copy of a contract from a purchasing agent, or you just want another bag of peanuts from a flight attendant, first say, "Can I ask you a favor?" Sound too easy? It's amazing how quickly and openly people respond to this by saying, "Sure." Suddenly, someone who would have otherwise been reluctant becomes receptive and helpful. This, of course, increases your chances of success when you need help.

Another way to soften your requests is to precede your questions with the phrase, "Is there any way..." Case in point: My wife Laura recently took our mini-van to the dealer's service center because the engine was making funny noises. Three hundred dollars later, we were the proud owners of a new fuel pump. The kicker was, our thirty-six month warranty had just expired—otherwise, the repair would have been fully covered. Fortunately, Laura is a savvy businessperson in her own right (or maybe she's just been around me too long). In any case, she was smart enough to ask, "Is there any way that this fuel pump repair, since the warranty just has expired, could still be covered by the manufacturer?"

The service representative said, "Usually, this would not be covered since your van is no longer under warranty, but let me make a few calls and see what I can do." Moments later, he was crediting Laura's American Express card. You go girl!

Lesson 46
Comfortable Isn't Always Most Effective

Years ago, when I started flying more frequently for business, I discovered that an interesting phenomenon occurs at the departure gate when an airline passenger checks in for their flight. When passengers ask gate agents about upgrade availability or flying stand-by, some gate agents process the request immediately, while others send the passenger away, saying, "Why don't you sit down until we call you." I have watched these interactions with interest, and I have noticed that experienced travelers respond differently to gate agents than casual vacation travelers.

Experienced business travelers don't go and sit down while the gate agents hand out seats. Instead, they stand close to the ticket counter, making sure the agent knows they are still there. By the time the flight actually leaves, most of the people who were hovering around the ticket counter are sitting comfortably on-board, while the less persistent passengers are left "sitting comfortably" in the gate area. At best, these more passive passengers end up getting stuffed into a middle seat in the rear of the airplane.

I believe that gate agents become very uncomfortable when a business traveler stands next to the counter—so they give them a seat to get rid of them. For those passengers who sit patiently waiting to be called, there's an old adage that says, "Out of sight, out of mind."

This same phenomenon occurs during sales calls. When a salesperson shows up for a two-o'clock appointment and the receptionist says, "Please have a seat," don't sit down. If you do, the receptionist's sense of urgency is lessened considerably. I have learned not to sit down. Instead, I say, "No thanks, I'll just stretch my legs for a few minutes until Mr. Smith is ready." Then I stand off to the side, but in plain view of the gatekeeper. (It's not hard to be in plain view at 6'6".)

I am not suggesting that you should become a pest. Standing nearby doesn't mean getting in the way or interrupting the flow of business. Be nice, polite, and cooperative. Just don't get too comfortable. In other words, don't go away. People work much harder to accommodate someone who is standing patiently, than someone who is content to just sit until they are called. Of course, when the prospect is ready to see you (or the gate agent upgrades you to first class,) that's when you sit down and make yourself comfortable.

Lesson 47
Take Your Coat Off and Stay Awhile

Nathan Barnett and his boss Glen came to my office a few months ago to sell me some life insurance. Nate had just broken into the insurance business with The Equitable Company, and Glen was his new sales manager. Both were decked out in pinstripe suits, white shirts, and designer ties, but since it was an office day for me, I was wearing khaki shorts and a golf shirt.

The meeting dragged on for ninety long minutes, well over the thirty minutes my friend Nate had requested to "practice" his sales presentation. Both men were very professional. In fact, maybe too professional. In my role as observer, I couldn't help but notice there was somewhat of a cultural imbalance, with two stiffly dressed salespeople in full business regalia, their coats on and ties tightly tied, and me sitting there in shorts and tennis shoes.

I found this experience particularly interesting because it represented the diametric opposite of my selling philosophy. In my view, stiff doesn't sell. When I meet with prospects, I always look for an opportunity to take my suit coat off as early as possible in the conversation. Politely, I say, "Mr. Prospect, would you mind if I take my coat off?" They always say it's fine, and most customers appreciate the reduction in formality.

> Contrary to the popular belief that salespeople should "dress for success," it's even more important to make potential buyers feel comfortable.

I usually try to time it so my coat comes off at some transition point in the meeting, either when the prospect and I are first sitting down, or when the meeting graduates from introductions to more specific business issues.

Contrary to the popular belief that salespeople should "dress for success," it's my view that it's even more important to make potential buyers feel comfortable. Suit coats tend to be stiff. They represent an emotional barrier that hides the real person underneath. Case in point, most salespeople don't wear their suit jackets when they are alone in their office. That's because they feel more comfortable without it. They also look more comfortable. You want to look and feel comfortable in front of your prospects and customers too, don't you?

Customers are rarely dressed to the hilt anyway. Even though they attend many important business meetings during the day, most of these meetings are conducted in shirtsleeves, and the only people who have suit coats on are the salespeople who come calling on the account.

I would much rather be on par with my prospects and customers, relaxed and comfortable and in a consultative mode, rather than a "sales" mode. I find it causes potential buyers to feel more relaxed and comfortable as well.

Taking your coat off also communicates a certain amount of expertise and experience. Young, inexperienced salespeople often try to hide behind a facade of professionalism. Real sales pros are less inhibited. Rather than worrying about trying to impress prospects with fine tailoring, they are anxious to get down to business, knowing the solutions they offer are far more important than the clothes they wear. In fact, shortly after I remove my coat in a meeting, I look for an opportunity to roll up my sleeves—because that's what experts do.

I have also noticed that sales calls tend to get longer when suit coats are off. If you ask permission to remove your coat, and your prospect says, "Sure, make yourself comfortable," your opportunity to sell expands significantly. Their permission essentially invites you to settle in and get ready for a more productive meeting. This strategy can easily turn a ten-minute sales call into a sixty-minute relationship-building opportunity.

As usual, there are a few cautions when applying this strategy. First, be aware that your customers are always watching. Therefore, I recommend against frivolously tossing your coat over the nearest chair. When customers see that you care about your own personal effects, they can feel more confident that you will care about theirs. There is no need to make a big deal. Simply ask for a hanger or fold your coat neatly and carefully place it off to the side.

Women also need to be careful, more than men. For all the reasons we have already discussed, it's OK for women to get comfortable in meetings too, but there is no need for a striptease. Being conservative is usually better.

Lastly, when you do get permission to take your coat off, leave it off. Some salespeople use their suit coats like a passport, putting it back on to make a trip to the men's room, for example. Unless you have secret note cards hidden in your jacket pockets, I would recommend leaving your coat alone for the duration of the meeting.

Only one time in my entire sales career did the customer not respond favorably to this. It was in mid-July while I was delivering a sales presentation to a large law firm in Miami. After the presentation kicked off, it was time to get serious and dive into the meat of our value proposition. Since everyone else in the audience was in shirt sleeves, I grabbed the lapels of my suit jacket and asked if anyone would mind if I took off my coat. Instantly, a hush fell over the meeting. Acting as spokesman, the senior partner explained that their firm had a policy that vendors had to keep their coats on during meetings. Can you believe it? There we were in the middle of the summer, in Miami, and these guys had a coat rule? But hey, it was their nickel. So, I kept my suit jacket on and continued the presentation. Shortly afterwards, I inconspicuously slipped my shoes off under the table and finished my entire presentation in stocking feet. I was pretty sure they didn't have a shoe rule. Two weeks later we were awarded the sale. Go figure.

Lesson 48
How to Kick Off an Interactive Sales Presentation

If I had a nickel for every sales presentation that got off on the wrong foot, Bill Gates and I would be much better friends. I am not referring to a problem with presentation skills like voice inflection, gesturing, or pace. These are important ingredients for effective sales presentations, but there are plenty of presentation skills trainers who can help you with these. Instead, I am talking about a different aspect of the presentation that very few people focus on. In my view, to maximize your effectiveness during a sales presentation, you must do something that will cause your presentation audience to become more receptive to your message.

At the very beginning of a sales presentation, it's a mistake for sellers to assume that since they have come to make a presentation, and the customer is there to attend a presentation, it's time to just "let the games begin." Once again, sellers have a certain tendency to want to jump right into an explanation of features and benefits, hoping (risking) that the audience will recognize value.

If I've said it once, I've said it a million times. Just because you (as a salesperson) have a great story to tell, doesn't mean prospects and customers will want to hear it. Similarly, just because people show up at your sales presentations, doesn't mean they are going to be attentive. Prospects already have lots on their minds. They have full calendars, lengthy to-do lists, and they are burdened with the daily challenges that arise in their respective businesses and in their personal lives.

Therefore, it is not surprising that prospects have limited attention spans when it comes to sales presentations, and it is up to the presenter to capture their interest and attention, or risk having value messages fall on deaf ears. What can you do to secure your audience's interest and attention? That depends on two things: who is in your audience, and what your objectives are for the sales presentation.

I should make the point that presentation audiences come in all shapes and sizes. Sometimes salespeople will present to prospective buyers in a one-on-one setting. Other times, the audience will be a decision committee with four, six, or even twelve people gathered in a conference room. Presenting to

> You must do something that will cause your presentation audience to become more receptive to your message.

large seminar audiences, as I often do, is yet another scenario. Either way, how you choose to manage yourself and your audience during the presentation will have a lot to do with the effectiveness of your message and the outcome of the sale.

Let's start by reviewing some sales presentation no-no's that may spare you a lot of grief later on in the sale.

Two Presentation Openings That Don't Work

Ironically, the most common opening sellers use to kick off their sales presentation is also the most problematic. I am referring to the scenario where a salesperson kicks his or her presentation off by projecting a prepared agenda onto the screen and saying, "My agenda for today's presentation is…"

This is how many salespeople are being trained. Every day,

presentation skills courses teach salespeople that to appear more professional when delivering sales presentations, they should begin with a prepared agenda for the meeting. In theory, opening a sales presentations with a prepared agenda might make you look more prepared. But, you have to ask yourself, what's the likelihood that every person who attends your sales presentation will all have the same agenda for the decision? It's more likely that your presentation audience will include different types of people with their own unique concerns, issues, and priorities.

In addition to having their own agendas for the decision, people will also have different expectations for your sales presentation. Consequently, sellers who open their presentations by saying, "My agenda for today is…," risk alienating some portion of their presentation audience. Do you think the audience cares about *your* agenda for the presentation? To gain audience buy-in, I recommend against opening your sales presentations with an agenda that will be instantly mismatched by some portion of your presentation audience.

At the opposite extreme, another risky way to open your sales presentation is to say, "Before we actually get started with the presentation, I would like to better understand your needs." Although I realize that many sellers are taught to kick off their presentations with open-ended questions in an attempt to foster interaction and uncover needs, this approach is often poorly received by skeptical buyer audiences. While some people do share valuable information, most prospects will remain silent, not wanting to share their thoughts, feelings, and concerns with a salesperson they don't yet know or trust. When this occurs, the silence can be deafening.

Recommendations for Opening a One-on-One Presentation

Kicking off a one-on-one sales presentation is easiest. Usually, you have talked with the prospect in advance, and you already have some feel for what they want you to cover. Even so, I recommend against jumping directly into the meat of your value proposition. Instead, here's a suggested opening sequence that I teach salespeople all over the world. This opening is designed to make audiences feel more at ease to ensure a more interactive meeting.

After some introductory banter, you initiate the discussion by saying:

Salesperson: "Mr. Prospect, when we talked last week via telephone, you brought up a number of different issues that were bothering you. I prepared some ideas to address these issues, but before I start barraging you with information, first let me ask, what would you like to accomplish in this meeting today?"

There isn't a prospect on the planet who won't appreciate your candor. They will also appreciate your preparedness and willingness to consider their input before you just blast forth. This technique alone can transform an average sales presentation into a powerful, mutual exchange of ideas.

Recommendations for Opening Group Presentations

Just like in the one-on-one presentation scenario, I recommend against jumping too quickly into the meat of your value proposition. Especially with decision committees, you have to expect a certain amount of internal politics and conflicting objectives. That's why it's so important to get audiences to buy into your credibility early in the presentation.

Here's a technique we teach in Question Based Selling to help sellers introduce their presentations and create a more receptive audience. After a few opening comments from your champion to set the stage for the meeting, you start your presentation by saying:

Salesperson: "Welcome everybody and thank you for your time today. Over the past month, I have had several conversations with John Benson (the meeting sponsor) about your upcoming deployment project. Although I don't know everything about your business, I am familiar with some of the challenges you currently face. That said, there are a couple ways we can proceed with this presentation.

On one hand, I could just deliver a generic corporate sales pitch. I have lots of Power-Point slides and I can talk really fast for a long period of time (smile). Or, if you would rather, we can roll up our sleeves and have a more in-depth conversation about your specific business issues. So, let me throw it out to the group: Would you rather see a generic slide presentation, or would you rather get into the details regarding your specific business environment?" (Be sure to pause for their response.)

In virtually every case, someone in the audience will immediately accept your invitation to get more specific. Second, everyone else will breathe a sigh of relief because they were thinking to themselves, "Thank you for not making us sit through another generic sales presentation!" Of course, their agreeing that it's OK to get more specific earns you the right to say, "In that case, can I ask a couple specific questions about your current environment?" This paves the way for you to open the dialogue by asking specific questions about their business, which gives you an opportunity to establish credibility, bond with the presentation audience, and cause them to become more receptive to your value messages.

Lesson 49
The Perils of Talking Too Much

Dale Carnegie observed many years ago that it is very difficult to learn about another person in a conversation if you are always talking. He was right. In fact, Tom Brezeale, of the Dale Carnegie Institute in Atlanta once told me, "When someone says that it doesn't bother them to speak in front of a group, it probably bothers the group." He was right, too!

Lesson 50
Flip Charts, White Boards, and Chalk-Talks

Lions and tigers and bears, oh my! I am reminded of the famous chant from *The Wizard of Oz* when I think about flip charts, white boards, and chalk-talks…oh my! If you are not already proficient at using these as communication vehicles, then pay attention because I am giving you an opportunity to significantly increase your sales.

There are only a few ways to communicate value in the sales process. One is to simply use words and verbally explain the points you want to make. By relying on words alone, however, you risk missing some opportunities because you are only tapping into one of the prospect's sensory functions—auditory. A salesperson's message can be enhanced significantly with visual aides. Perhaps you have heard the phrase that a picture is worth a thousand words. This is definitely true in sales, as prospects and customers can absorb lots of visual information very quickly. In addition, visual aides that are well crafted can enhance your credibility and give your verbal explanations a much better perspective.

When delivering sales presentations, the most common visual aides salespeople use are product brochures and prepared slides. But these aren't necessarily the most productive in terms of communicating value. Why not? Because a vast majority of sales presenters use similar-looking product brochures and prepared slides—in which case, if you do the same thing as everyone else, you will only forfeit your competitive edge.

PowerPoint slides especially have been overused, particularly in the corporate arena. How many PowerPoint slides do you think the average decision-maker in a large prospect account sees in a typical month? I don't have the answer because our researchers are still counting. 'Death by PowerPoint' has even become an inside joke among audiences who have had to sit through hundreds of standard slide show presentations. Borrrr...ing!

> 'Death by PowerPoint' has become an inside joke among audiences who have had to sit through hundreds of standard slide show presentations.

If you really want to differentiate yourself and the solutions you offer, then I would suggest drawing your own pictures. Many sales are won (or lost) during the sales presentation, and your ability to communicate value is critical to your success in selling. Communicating value is an interesting concept, however. Prospects will be forming their impressions about your products and services, but even more importantly, they will be forming an impression about you. Just because a salesperson has glossy brochures or fancy slides, however, doesn't mean they will be viewed as credible in the eyes of their prospects.

When I'm the buyer, I want to know that I am dealing with someone who knows what they are talking about. I can read the sales propaganda and presentation slides by myself. What I really want is someone who can translate generic product information into a customized solution that will meet my specific needs. Essentially, I want to be dealing with an expert.

Have you ever gone into a local hardware store with a Mr.

Fix-it type problem that you didn't know how to solve? When the first person you ask gives you a weak answer, you look for a second opinion. The second person you ask provides such a verbosely detailed explanation that you have no idea what they said. Finally, a third person whips out some paper and draws a picture. Suddenly everything makes sense! That's how customers often feel in a sales presentation. Ultimately, they need you to make your proposed solutions make sense.

You can significantly increase your value in the eyes of your prospects by effectively using flip charts, white boards, and chalk-talks to communicate key points in your sales presentations. I would even argue that marker pens are one of the most powerful tools a salesperson has at their disposal to communicate value. Illustrating key points with pictures gives you the advantage of creating visual representations that customers can easily understand and remember. The person holding the marker pen also has a unique opportunity to enhance his or her credibility by leading a more productive forum for discussion. Even better, when all the presentation slides have been packed back into the salesperson's briefcase, the drawings that were made will still be there on the flip chart or white board, and can be referred to later when answering questions or reiterating key messages.

Even at informal meetings, sellers should always have a pad of paper and pen handy to make notes and illustrate important concepts when it's appropriate in the discussion. In smaller, more intimate settings, I often tear off a few flip chart pages and lay them flat on the conference table like a placemat. This gives me the opportunity to lead a chalk-talk discussion (on the paper) without having to get up from the table.

Another idea is to hand the marker pen to your customer and ask them to draw pictures. Since people love to talk about themselves and their business environments, you would be amazed at how fast the white board fills up with important information—that is, if you are willing to hand over the pen.

You might even change the way you ask for meetings. Most salespeople who initiate contact with new prospects are hoping to get an appointment. Essentially, they want to sit down with potential buyers to build a relationship that will ultimately turn into a sale. From the prospect's perspective, however, many buyers don't have time to "sit down" and build relationships with salespeople. That's why I don't ask for meetings. Instead, when it's time to close for an appointment, I ask, "Mr. Prospect, given your upcoming projects, would it make sense for us to get in front of a white board and have a more specific conversation about how our solutions would impact your business?"

Asking to get in front of a white board is an extremely productive closing question. When prospects are asked for appointments, they tend to assume that a one-hour meeting will consist of forty-five minutes of fluff and only fifteen minutes (or less) of meat. Asking to get in front of a white board, however, communicates a greater sense of value because the implication suggests a more in-depth discussion and a better use of the prospect's time.

I tell audiences that one of the leading indicators of a salesperson's capability is being able to deliver a full product presentation without the help of any sales collateral (slides or brochures). Frankly, I have never met a top performer in sales who didn't excel at the white board. That goes for managers too. We must realize that much of the sales process takes place outside of the formal presentation (i.e. on notepads and sometimes even on bar napkins). So, the lesson here is clear—if you learn to be a good chalk-talker, your credibility will increase significantly. So will your sales results.

Lesson 51
Your Volume Speaks Volumes

To some people, the stereotypical salesman sounds a lot like a carnival barker—loud and brash, hoping to entice prospective customers to come over and partake in random games of chance. But if you study the more consistent, top performing salespeople at companies all over the globe, you will notice that they are usually not loud and brash. In fact, these top performers are oftentimes quite reserved. Rather than rant and rave about their solutions, they tend to speak with a certain quiet confidence, and customers tend to listen.

Speaking in a loud voice often times is an attempt to project an air of confidence that will hopefully impress other people. But loudness is usually a tell-tale sign of insecurity. That's why some of the least effective people are also some of the biggest talkers. In Texas, they characterize this as, "Having a big hat, but not much cattle."

Truth be told, loudness tends to push other people away. You can test this out for yourself. The next time you are talking with someone in your office or on the golf course, turn up your volume a few notches and watch their body language. People begin to recoil almost instantly. Suddenly you will seem too close, too overbearing, and their congeniality will quickly be replaced by a greater sense of resistance. Rather than bonding with the person you are talking with, your loudness will push them away, and it doesn't matter whether you are actually feeling confident or not.

> Top performers tend to speak with a certain quiet confidence, and customers tend to listen.

Ironically, sales professionals can project a greater sense of confidence by talking softly and more deliberately. Simply by lowering your voice, you draw people in closer as opposed to pushing them away. While it will always be necessary to emphasize key points, if you make a conscious effort to speak with a quiet confidence, your volume will speak volumes about you.

Lesson 52
People Need Time to Adjust

Younger salespeople tend to be aggressive and hard-charging, and that will probably always be the case. But as my own business career has matured, I have noticed that the pace with which I deliver information and ideas has slowed down.

When I was younger and felt well prepared for a meeting or presentation, I had a tendency to jump into every conversation with both guns blazing, full of ideas, suggestions, and recommendations. But as you might guess, my ideas were often met with a certain amount of resistance because my audience wasn't always ready to accept the changes I was proposing.

What happens if your prospects and customers are not yet ready to accept your ideas? You could push harder and harder, and be even more emphatic, hoping that your conviction will somehow help to sway them. In sales, however, the harder you push, the harder your prospects and customers will tend to push back. Therefore, instead of pushing harder and harder, you will find that people are more likely to be receptive when they are given some time to get used to your ideas.

Think of the customer's ideas as their friends, and your ideas as your friends. With that in mind, you can't just expect prospects and customers to drop their old friends and replace them with your friends, no matter how good yours seem. Instead, you must give them some time to adjust. Therefore, my advice is simple—slow down. It gives other people a chance to consider their alternatives and have your ideas become their new friends.

Lesson 53
Ask for an Inch... Get a Mile

Back in my territory selling days, the ideal scenario was to gather all the key players involved in a decision together in a room for a one and a half to two hour sales presentation. Since I was evangelizing new technology, my presentation was structured to create a certain snowball effect. Many of the points I wanted to make required some time to set up. But whenever I asked prospects for two full hours of their time, they thought I was nuts. Prospects don't want to dedicate that much of their day to a single vendor, especially one trying to penetrate into a new account. As a result, I usually got an hour, which in many cases, turned out to last much less than 60 minutes.

Have you ever noticed how a one-hour presentation scheduled to begin at 9:00am never starts on time? By the time the attendees straggle in and everyone gets settled, the clock has ticked forward 10 minutes or so. The usual pleasantries are exchanged, followed by introductions, and the presentation doesn't actually begin until 9:15am. Of course, you also have to allow ten minutes or so at the end of your presentation for Q & A and to discuss possible next steps. If you do the math, you will find that this one-hour scenario only leaves the salesperson a little more than thirty minutes to explain an hour's worth of presentation material.

> Have you ever noticed how a one-hour presentation scheduled to begin at 9:00am never starts on time?

This shrinking window has caused sellers and marketers to invest tremendous amounts of energy trying to figure out how salespeople can be more effective when there isn't enough time. In my opinion, this is a miss. Trying to figure out ways to communicate your value proposition in small windows of time is not the answer. Instead, the goal should be to secure larger chunks of the prospect's time, knowing that more time gives you more opportunities to uncover needs and communicate value.

If you need more time but don't feel comfortable asking for two full hours, then try doing what I did. Rather than ask for a single hour, I used to ask for an hour and fifteen minutes. In my experience, it was relatively easy to ask for and secure an extra fifteen minutes of the prospect's time. I explained that this would give us enough time for what-if scenarios and questions. This extra time gave me a strategic advantage when it came to delivering the actual presentation.

Don't let the subtlety of this request mask its significance. On the surface, the extra fifteen minutes gives you some valuable breathing room at the end of your presentation. What it also does (and here's the significant part) is clear the prospect's calendar for two full hours. Most people schedule appointments to begin at the top of the hour. Therefore, if your presentation begins at 1:00pm, and you succeeded in getting the prospect to block off an hour and fifteen minutes, they probably won't schedule their next meeting until 3:00pm. Now, while your competition is having to condense their sales presentations into a thirty-minute window, you have already cleared the way to run over your allotted time if the presentation is going well.

Lesson 54
Are You Good with Names?

Why do people have a terrible time remembering names? I, myself, used to be horrible with names. I could walk onto a tennis court or into a business meeting, introduce myself, shake three or four people's hands, and seconds later, not remember anyone's name. Granted, I'm probably not the smartest egg in the carton, but I'm not the dumbest either! Needless to say, not being able to remember people's names is a shortcoming that can create some very awkward situations.

Now, as I travel all over the world working with sales organizations to increase their selling effectiveness, I constantly hear complaints from salespeople that they can remember faces and telephone numbers, but they can't remember names. The kicker is, if you cannot remember someone's name, they know you don't know. Your expression and mannerisms will give you away every time. Isn't that odd? Sellers want to have mutually beneficial strategic relationships with prospects and customers, but they can't even remember their names.

Years ago, I was lamenting to my longtime friend Richard Sites about not being good with names. Richard listened to me complain for several minutes, and then he calmly asked if I would like to solve this problem. Frankly, I would have undergone brain surgery to be able to remember names better! So, of course I said, "Sure I want to solve the problem!"

That's when Richard gave me some simple but valuable advice. Now I have what some people might say is a photographic memory for names. It's uncanny. At the beginning of our "live" QBS training programs, we usually start by going around the room and having people introduce themselves. During these introductions, I make it a point to remember everyone's name. Even when there are fifty or sixty people in the audience, I want to call on course participants by name, which increases interaction and fosters a more intimate training experience. Nowadays, people come up to me and ask, "How in the world do you remember everyone's name?"

Richard taught me many years ago that my memory capability was not the problem. I mean, you can rattle off your home telephone number without hesitation, can't you? What about your social security number? Children's birth dates? Last year's W2? If you can remember these things, then you are not physically deficient in terms of your memory ability. For most people, the reason they don't remember names is because they have a technique problem with how they assimilate and store people's names. Let me explain.

During a typical introduction, particularly when meeting someone for the first time, people tend to think more about themselves than the other person. They worry about their facial expression, maintaining eye contact, and making sure they say their own name correctly. It's natural to be thinking about yourself since first impressions are very important. And if you've ever flubbed an introduction by slurring your words, speaking out of turn, or grabbing the wrong part of someone's hand, it's understandable that you would be a little self-conscious, wanting to make sure you don't flub another one.

Open Your Input Valve

I am living proof that you can dramatically improve your memory for names using a simple two-part strategy. The first step involves making a conscious effort to open your input valve. What's an input valve? It's your ability to focus on and receive information from the other person, rather than focusing attention on yourself. Most people, when they meet others, focus on themselves. But if you are thinking about yourself, your posture, or your enunciation during an introduction, then you are not thinking about the other person. As a result, this important piece of information never makes it into your brain, in which case, you won't remember their name. Therefore, if you believe that names are important, you must make a conscious effort to focus your attention on the other person. By changing your focus, you allow this information to get into your noggin, and you accomplish eighty percent of your objective right there.

To further the point, Richard let me in on a little secret. He says that if you've been out in the business world for any length of time, whether you think you are bumbling the introduction or you are feeling really suave, people you meet for the first time

> The key is to focus on the other person's name long enough to input it into your brain.

will likely perceive you the same way. Therefore, if it doesn't help to think about yourself, why not focus your attention on something more important—like the other person's name? The key is to focus on their name long enough to input it into your brain. If you don't hear or you don't understand someone's name when they introduce themselves, ask them to repeat it. Most people will appreciate the fact that their name is important to you.

Burn Their Names Into Your Memory for Easy Recall

Once you have "mentally ingested" this critical piece of information (i.e. the person's name), you must burn it into your memory for recall later. This is the second step in the process of having a great memory for names.

As humans, we have a capacity for remembering those things that get burned into our memories. I'm sure you remember embarrassing moments from the past, for example, or special occasions, because these have been burned into your memory. If we apply this same logic to names, you will find that your ability to remember someone's name will increase significantly after it gets "burned" into your memory.

How do you burn someone's name into your memory? Here's an analogy to illustrate the point. Back in the days of tight pants, ponytails, and muscle cars, it used to be cool for high school kids to stomp on the gas at a green light and peel out in their cars. Some people call it burning rubber. Of course, doing this leaves wide black tire marks on the road as a long-lasting impression of a few moments' bravado. You can leave long-lasting impressions on the human brain as well if you make a conscious effort to focus on, and burn into your memory, specific pieces of information that are worth remembering (names, in this case).

When I introduce myself to someone in a professional setting, I usually extend my hand and say, "Hi, I'm Tom Freese with QBS Research." Then, I listen carefully as the other person responds, saying, "Hi Tom, I'm Jane Smith of Scientific Atlanta." First, I make an effort to pay attention so my input valve is open and her name gets into my brain. Then, I consciously focus on her name for a few seconds, long enough to burn it into my memory.

"Jane… Smith….," I think to myself. Got it!

Being good with names does not have to be difficult. But it may require an adjustment on your part to take the focus off of yourself and put it on other people. What's the alternative? Wouldn't it seem odd to you, as a customer, if a salesperson wanted to establish a strategic business relationship with you, but they couldn't even remember your name?

Lesson 55

Big Points for Defusing Customer Problems

When I joined Baxter's Systems Division in 1987, I inherited a virtual hornet's nest at Hialeah Hospital in Miami, Florida. My predecessor in the account apparently had a falling-out with hospital administration, and it was now my job to clean up the mess.

After some finagling, I secured an introductory appointment with a reluctant Chief Financial Officer. When I showed up at his office, he had gathered his entire staff into the adjoining conference room, and they were well-armed to defend their position on recent problems. I was prepared as well. But rather than jumping right into the foxhole for some hand-to-hand combat, I wanted them to know I was there as a peacemaker.

"I understand there were some problems in the past, and I've heard about it in bits and pieces," I started. "My primary objective here today is to understand where we are in the account, so any outstanding issues with Baxter Corporation can be appropriately addressed."

With that, Hialeah Hospital's administrative staff came alive. Everyone, it seemed, was unhappy. I opened my notebook and started writing notes about what they said. This complaint session seemed to take a natural progression as we went clockwise around the table. The CFO spoke last, reiterating some of the earlier points that had already been made. But after all the dust had settled, Hialeah Hospital's unhappiness netted out into two basic issues:

a.) Administration wanted more control over the delivery timetable for new systems Baxter was under contract to provide.

b.) Because Hialeah Hospital had been a long-time customer, they felt they deserved a certain priority status over smaller and potentially less loyal Baxter customers.

Both requests seemed reasonable from my perspective, and given that Baxter and Hialeah both wanted to continue a business relationship, there was nothing on the table that a little proactive communication couldn't resolve.

> Customer problems tend to get larger when emotions are running high.

This brings us to the most important lesson in dealing with customer problems; which is, customer problems tend to get larger when emotions are running high. Dealing with customer problems is part of managing the sales process. But to deal with problems effectively, you must dig down into the issue far enough to understand the actual problem. And the key to success starts with letting people fully express their point of view. Most problems, after the customer has had a chance to vent their frustrations, aren't nearly as big or bad as they originally seemed. The good news for salespeople is, you still get big points for understanding and then resolving the customer's problem.

Most customer problems are the result of some form of miscommunication, plain and simple. In essence, you can't solve a problem you don't understand. Likewise, customers are not going to be happy with a solution they don't understand. In short, sellers who willingly accept the role of mediator within their accounts are much more likely to succeed than those who take on the role of combatant.

Lesson 56
Some Rules Were Meant to be Broken

Terry Macaleer was the Vice President of Sales when I was at Shared Medical Systems (SMS). Terry was a no-nonsense guy who didn't have much patience with the traditional corporate bureaucracy. He was more interested in maintaining a customer-centric focus. In fact, Terry used to tell us, "If you are ever in a situation where something needs to get done, and you have presented the facts to management, but you still can't get the approvals necessary to do what's right for the customer, then change the facts!"

We all live and work in a rules-based society. To avoid chaos, parents have rules for raising their children; schools have rules that govern the student body; and companies establish rules to help the organization stay focused on important business objectives. Rules are created to serve as guidelines for the masses. But it is not realistic to expect that a set of guidelines will address every possible situation that could arise. That's why I agree with Terry by arguing that the salesperson is ultimately responsible for doing what's right for the company. They are also responsible for doing what's right for the customer. In that vein, sellers take on the role of professional mediators who are working to bring two sides together into a mutually beneficial business transaction.

As an example of this, when I sold technology products (hardware and software), customers were always looking to reduce their risk of making a bad decision. But no matter how many references and success stories we provided, pulling the trigger on the decision still required a certain leap of faith.

> "I will make you this guarantee. If our product does not do what we said it would do, I will take it back at no cost to you."

That's why I used to say to customers, "I will make you this guarantee. If our product does not do what we said it would do, I will take it back at no cost to you."

The first time my manager heard me say this to a prospective customer, he went crazy. "You don't have the authority to say that!" he exclaimed.

Au contraire, I will always hold the belief that if a product doesn't do what the sales team said it would do, it should absolutely be returnable at no cost to the buyer. Misleading prospects does not lead to long-term success.

Customers would ask, "Are you willing to put your guarantee in writing?"

"Absolutely," I would confidently respond. "To avoid any miscommunication about our product's capabilities, however, I first would ask you (Mr. Customer) to document exactly what your requirements are in terms of what you need the product to do, and I will then sign off that our product will indeed perform as required."

Some customers would immediately prepare a document that reflected their needs. I would have my systems engineer review their requirements to make sure we could meet or exceed expectations, and then sign off. If for some reason they expected more than our product could deliver, I would bring any discrepancies to their attention and make sure we were all on the same page.

Frankly, most customers didn't take the time to create a requirements document. With the credibility I had earned thus far in the sales process, and my willingness to stand behind what we were saying about our solution's capabilities, my reassurance was often all prospective buyers needed to feel comfortable enough to move forward with a purchase.

> Sellers take on the role of professional mediators who are working to bring two sides together into a mutually beneficial business transaction.

I am not encouraging renegade behavior or suggesting that you should go out and break the rules of your company. I am saying, however, that when a special circumstance in one of your accounts calls for an exception to what would otherwise be considered standard practice, it is your responsibility as a salesperson to mediate the situation in a way that will accomplish the mutual objective. Sometimes that means adapting the rules to match the situation.

Lesson 57
Business Entertainment:
A Necessary Evil?

Countless business deals have been consummated over drinks, during dinner, or while on the golf course. But the competitive advantage that comes from business entertainment remains unclear. The act of "wining and dining" potential buyers will always be part of the selling landscape, but it is a mistake to assume that whoever wines and dines the customer most, will win the sale.

In my view, the real significance of business entertainment is that it creates opportunities to spend time with prospects and customers. Inviting prospects to dinner, for example, is a good way to get them off-line and away from the hustle and bustle of their daily routines. It's also a good way to include upper management and others who may impact the decision. A key executive, for example, who is not available to attend your 2:00pm meeting may be very interested in meeting you for dinner at a nice restaurant. Entertaining customers is especially valuable when it causes them to relax, because people who are relaxed tend to share more information about their needs and where you stand in the sale. Of course, you gain a competitive advantage when prospects choose to openly share.

Business entertainment also serves as a breeding ground for personal relationships. There is no magic formula here. Buyers will tend to gravitate to those with whom they feel most comfortable. Just by swapping a few personal stories, you can establish a rapport that will ultimately transform itself into a mutual respect between buyers and sellers.

There is a potential downside to business entertainment, however. For example, one of the worst things a salesperson can do is lure prospects into a social situation and then pummel them with features and benefits. Most decision-makers have already had the unfortunate experience of being held captive on the golf course or over dinner, while an unrelenting salesperson reiterates their value proposition. If the prospect wants to talk business the entire time, fine. But unless dinner is your only opportunity to communicate value, it's better to save the meat of your corporate presentation for the prospect's conference room and use entertainment for establishing rapport and building relationships.

> People who are relaxed tend to share more information about their needs and more information about where you stand in the sale.

Be ready, though. The conversation will turn to business at some point, which will give you an opportunity to position your solution against other competing alternatives.

A good rule of thumb for business entertainment is this: if you want to use entertainment to consummate business deals, then you must be the consummate host. The consummate host focuses on those things that are most important to their guests, and they are also excellent listeners. It only stands to reason that you won't learn much about your prospects and customers if you are doing all the talking. But if you listen long enough and hard enough to what potential buyers are saying, they will eventually tell you exactly where you stand in the opportunity and what must happen for you to win the sale.

Frankly, I did very little extravagant business entertainment in my own corporate selling career. I enjoy a nice dinner or golf outing as much as the next guy, but I tended to gravitate away from entertaininment as a rule because it took up such large chunks of the business day. Being on the golf course for five or six hours with one customer meant that I was unavailable to work with many other customers. In fact, rather than trying to "woo" prospective buyers into giving me their business, I usually reserved entertainment to be used as more of a celebration after consummating a deal. I liked taking customers out for golf or a nice dinner as a way to celebrate the new partnership. In fact, just before I closed the largest deal of my sales career, my contacts at Delta Air Lines teased me one day during lunch saying, "Tom, your competitors are picking us up in stretch limousines and taking us to the nicest restaurants in Atlanta, and here we are with you eating chicken sandwiches at Chick-fil-a."

Everyone laughed and my champion at Delta Air Lines even accused me of being cheap. But guess what? In terms of building relationships, credibility, and trust, it's amazing how much can be accomplished when everyone on the decision committee is huddled around a small table in a fast food joint.

Lesson 58
A Kernel of Wisdom about Giving Advice

Offering advice to someone is always a touchy subject. So, let me give you a kernel of wisdom that may help. If you are going to offer your advice, it's a good idea to first walk a mile in the other person's shoes. That way, when you actually give the advice, you're a mile away and you have their shoes…

Lesson 59
Be Detail-Oriented to Increase Your Credibility

Telling prospects that your company has had some recent product announcements is less impactful than saying, "Mr. Prospect, we've had thirteen new announcements in the last three and a half months, two of which may directly affect your business." Being more descriptive with your words has a greater impact because being detail-oriented increases your credibility.

If you are a salesperson, your words should be descriptive enough to paint pictures of value in the customer's mind. Of course, the clearer the pictures are that you paint, the easier it is to get potential buyers excited about purchasing your product or service. I'm not talking about a whimsical concept here, rather I am talking about the height of professionalism. You would want your doctor and your attorney to be specific and detail-oriented, wouldn't you? Then, why shouldn't sales professionals be detail-oriented too, to communicate the same high levels of competence, credibility, and professionalism?

Being detail-oriented is not difficult, but it does need to be practiced. For example, consider the following passage:

"On a cold, damp Thursday evening back in the fall of 1987, the temperature outside had already dropped into the low 40's, and the rain fell steadily into the night. Suddenly, at 2:30am, Mr. Stephens awoke to the faint but continuous ticking of his bedside clock. "

If you are a salesperson, your words should be descriptive enough to paint pictures of value in the customer's mind.

This passage has been excerpted from a short story to illustrate a key point. The author could have simply said, "Mr. Stephens woke up in the night and heard the clock." But creative writers use detail to form vivid images that will tell believable and captivating stories, in order to communicate their messages. So do top salespeople. Try it for yourself. The next time you reference your existing customer base, don't just say, "We have the largest marketshare in the industry." While this isn't wrong, it isn't nearly as powerful as saying, "We currently support over 750 customers representing a variety of different industries including healthcare, manufacturing, financial services, tele-communications, and technology. In fact, if we continue growing at our current pace, our customer base will double in the next fifteen months."

Since every prospect and customer you engage will be forming an impression about your credibility, why not use details to communicate a greater sense of value and give them something they can really sink their teeth into?

Lesson 60
Is it Possible to Be Too Honest?

You should not have to breach your integrity to be successful in sales. This has always been a foundational part of my philosophy on sales. In fact, I will go one step further to say that it's my opinion that someone who breaches his or her integrity doesn't deserve to win the sale.

Integrity plays an important role in the selling profession. Most sellers know this implicitly. When buyers and sellers come together to form mutually beneficial business relationships, they forge certain bonds of trust that mustn't be compromised if the relationship is to prosper long term.

But be careful not to take this need to 'be honest' to an extreme. Some sellers (believe it or not) take it upon themselves to try and make up for all the less-than-honest salespeople by being more than honest. Sales engineers, too, seem to have adopted the battle cry, "I am going to tell customers the whole truth and nothing but the truth."

Well, guess what? There are different degrees of being honest. For example, imagine what might happen if a Volvo salesperson approached a young couple in a dealer showroom asking, "How can I help you today?"

"We're interested in this model here," the couple replies.

"This is our SR70 sport sedan," the salesperson says. "It's a great car. In fact, only 162 people were killed or maimed in this model last year!"

One of the most compelling reasons to buy Volvo is safety. But while this information about number of fatalities in a Volvo might represent a significant advantage over other automobiles in its class, painting such a gruesome picture may not be the best way to start a sales conversation.

Every product or service being offered has certain strengths, and also, weaknesses. While I agree that sellers should be forthright about their strengths and their weaknesses, perhaps it goes without saying that an honest salesperson who focuses on his or her product's strengths will outsell the honest salesperson who focuses more on weaknesses.

The lesson here is simple. The desire to be honest should be a given, but it does not replace the need to be smart in how your product or service is positioned.

Lesson 61
To Be More Successful in Business... Get Personal

Prospects receive so much junk in the mail nowadays that advertisements, form letters, and invitations to upcoming events are virtually useless. In fact, the sheer volume of mail has increased to the point that people open their mail next to a trash can so they can immediately discard everything that fails to grab their attention. But sending information through the mail is still one of the best ways to communicate with prospects and customers—given that you can differentiate yourself and your messages from all the other junk.

The key to differentiating your communications is to personalize your message. Personalized messages will always take priority over the usual junk mail. Sending out professionally printed invitations, for example, isn't nearly as impactful as sending those same invitations after you have written a small personal note on the inside. Even when sending product literature, attaching a personal note or adding a simple 'P.S.' on the bottom of your cover letter can differentiate you from the other junk mail prospects won't even bother to read. Handwriting the words, "Jim, this is important!" on the outside of the envelope can also make a big difference.

The same is true when leaving voice-mail messages or sending email. If your personality and/or sense of humor comes across in the messages you send, prospects and customers are

> Personalized messages will always take priority over the usual junk mail.

much more likely to respond. They are beginning to form a relationship with you—whether they like it or not.

Personalizing your communications is one of the simplest adjustments sellers can make to increase their productivity. Nonetheless, naysayers will still complain that taking time to personalize every letter or message requires lots of extra work. I say, this is a narrow view. Sure, being strategic requires a certain proactive effort, but it can pay off in big ways. To me, extra work is all the selling effort that gets expended without ever being noticed by qualified prospects.

My Greatest Selling Success Was Very Personal

My single greatest sale didn't occur in the boardroom of a large corporation. Rather, it was the result of a letter-writing campaign I created to nominate my wife Laura as an Olympic torch bearer leading up to the 1996 Summer Olympic Games in Atlanta.

On a flight back from Ft. Myers, Florida in February 1996, I noticed an article in *USA Today* reporting that the nominations for torch bearers had just been closed, after receiving some 30,000 applications. Frankly, I wasn't even aware the Olympic Torch Committee was accepting applications, but I knew instantly who deserved a nomination.

As soon as I got off the airplane, I telephoned the contact person listed in the article. After a brief conversation, it was clear that she couldn't help me because the nominations had officially been closed.

It was time to test my letter-writing skills. Fortunately, words flowed easily for me that night as I crafted the most impactful letter I have ever written, nominating Laura to carry the torch in the upcoming Olympics. Since the official nominations were closed, I didn't bother sending the letter through the standard channels. Instead, I sent the letter to a powerful list of business and political leaders in the Southeast including Georgia Governor Zell Miller, Former Speaker of the House Newt Gingrich, Ted Turner, Atlanta Mayor Bill Campbell, and Douglas Ivester, President of Coca-Cola (sponsor of the Olympic Torch Relay).

In the letter, I wrote that nineteen months earlier, Laura had been diagnosed with cancer. But rather than give in to this disease, she decided to fight, and through her incredible spirit and determination, Laura prevailed. "She didn't receive any medals for her victory over cancer," I wrote in the letter, "but with your help, the honor of being selected to carry the Olympic torch would hold Laura up as an inspiration to everyone else who may come to a similar fork in the road."

The challenge was, if I had just sent the letter by itself,

none of these people would have responded. They probably wouldn't have even read the letter. Important people like these are surrounded by all kinds of handlers who open their mail and screen their calls. In fact, I assumed that a junior staff person would probably open my letter, and reply with a pre-fabricated form letter. That is, unless I did something out of the ordinary, which is right up my alley.

"What could I do to ensure that each of these political and business icons would personally receive and read my letter?" I wondered. The answer was, I had to get personal. Therefore, on each letter, I paper clipped a family photograph—our Christmas picture from the previous year. I did this figuring that a handler wouldn't be so quick to throw away a personal photograph. This would at least ensure that my letter would make it past the gatekeeper. Additionally, I crafted the opening sentence of the letters I sent to sound personal. For example, in the letter I wrote to Ted Turner, I said, "Dear Mr. Turner, Although we have come close over the years, we haven't actually met. But since I know you are a no-bull guy, this is a no-bull letter."

Did they read my letters? I have no way of knowing what actually transpired after my letters were mailed, but within a week, the Chairman's office of Coca-Cola personally called Laura and invited her to honor them by carrying the Olympic torch on the way to the stadium, on the day of the opening ceremonies.

As I wrote in the preface of my first book, "tears flowed again that day when Laura hoisted the Olympic Flame, in front of 20,000 cheering fans, as a symbol that reflected her own personal victory, having faced the ultimate personal challenge." Thank you Governor Miller, Speaker Gingrich, Mr. Turner, Mayor Campbell, and Mr. Ivester...for reading my letter.

Lesson 62
The Sale Ain't Over, Until It's Over

Yogi Berra, the famous major league baseball hall-of-famer, coined a now-familiar phrase by saying, "It ain't over, 'til it's over." Basically, he was suggesting that you should never let your guard down until the contest has completely ended. Even if you are several runs ahead with two outs in the bottom of the ninth, the opposing team can still come back and win the game. This can also happen in sales. Even after you have been selected vendor-of-choice and everything seems to be moving in the right direction, the deal can still be lost if you relax and let your competitors back into the picture. Unfortunately, I had to learn this the hard way in my career.

In 1994, my company was one of four vendor finalists competing for a large technology implementation at the Southern Company, a very prestigious corporate account in downtown Atlanta. After a vigorous evaluation, we were selected vendor-of-choice. My team was overjoyed and we spent the next few days celebrating. Unbeknownst to us, one of our competitors spent those next few days selling. And they succeeded in raising enough fear, uncertainty, and doubt with key players in the account that the decision process was halt-ed and the evaluation was re-opened. In fact, the tables were turned so dramatically that we had to compete more vigorously than ever just to stay in the game.

Four months later, after another exhaustive battle, we were once again selected as Southern Company's preferred vendor. This time, however, we did not let our guards down until the deal was completely closed.

The most valuable lesson I took away from this experience was the realization that salespeople are notoriously bad losers. Whenever multiple vendors are competing for a single piece of

> With nothing to lose, desperate competitors will do everything they can to disrupt your sale.

business, especially in a large strategic deal, the selected vendor will likely be ecstatic, and the other vendors who are not going to win the deal will likely be incensed. "They're making a huge mistake," each of the non-selected vendors will think. And with nothing to lose, desperate competitors will try anything to get back into your accounts, and if they succeed, they will do everything they can to disrupt your sale.

Part of your job as a salesperson is to prevent competitors from getting back in the account once you have been selected as vendor-of-choice. Keeping them out requires a proactive effort on your part, however. This means preparing customers in advance for potential acts of desperation from those who may not be happy about the impending decision.

So here are a few proactive strategies you can use to beat competitors to the punch and derail any last-ditch efforts they might try to get back into your accounts.

Prepare Your Prospects for Battle

Soon after thanking the prospect for selecting you as vendor-of-choice, I recommend that you spend a few minutes giving them a dose of perspective. "Be aware, Mr. Prospect, that the other vendors involved in this selection process are not going to be happy with your decision. In their minds, you are making a big mistake, and while I don't know these individuals, some salespeople will do anything to stop the decision from moving forward."

I say this to the customers because it prepares them for battle. No one wants to be told they are making a mistake, especially not by a vendor who has nothing to lose and might try to sabotage the prospect's intended direction.

Leverage "What if" Scenarios

Another way to prepare prospects for possible last-ditch competitive advances is to ask a few key "what if" questions. "Mr. Prospect, what if the salesperson from the competing vendor tries to circumvent your authority by going directly to your boss?" Just the suggestion of this will make many customers cringe. What do you think will happen, then, if your competitor actually tries this tactic?

Or, you might ask, "Ms. Prospect, how will your implementation timeframe be affected if one of the other vendors succeeds in disrupting your decision and delaying the purchase a few more weeks?" Once again, a decision-maker can't hear this without feeling the hair on the back of their necks stand up.

Sour Any Special Deals in Advance

Speaking of "what if" scenarios, I would also ask, "Mr. Prospect, what happens if one of the other vendors comes back with a 'special offer' as a way to get you to reverse course?" You might as well be proactive and pose the question because this scenario is likely to happen. Remember that your competitors at this point have nothing to lose.

The key is making your competitor's last-ditch offer seem less special before it ever gets offered. You can easily accomplish this by planting a seed of skepticism with your prospects. For example, I might address this issue by saying, "Mr. Prospect, you might want to beware of any last minute bait-and-switch offers. You and I both know that companies aren't in business to lose money. Therefore, if one of the vendors you didn't select comes back with a special deal, if it is real, why didn't they propose it earlier?"

Preventing other vendors from re-entering your deals can have a lot to do with your success in sales. When competitors sense even the slightest opportunity to disrupt your sale, they will be ruthless in their efforts. If, however, you are proactive in shutting down their advances, you can significantly increase your probability of success in completing the transaction. Perhaps Yogi Berra knew as much about professional sales as he did baseball, because in selling, the sale is definitely not over until it's over.

Lesson 63
Neutralize Your Anti-Champions

Internal champions are people within your accounts who are willing to fight for your product or service because they are convinced you offer the best solution. For obvious reasons, salespeople spend tremendous amounts of time trying to create internal champions within their large corporate accounts. Salespeople should spend just as much time worrying about the threat posed by the anti-champions within these same accounts. What do I mean by anti-champions? Basically, the anti-champion is the person who doesn't want you to win the sale. For whatever reason, they would rather support some other alternative and are actively campaigning against your proposed solution.

The most common type of anti-champion is the person who supports your competitor's solution. Sometimes these people have had positive results with another product in the past, in which case, people tend to gravitate toward solutions that are most familiar. It could also be that they had a bad experience with your company, which might cause them to have a negative bias against you. Or, it could just be that they are extremely budget-conscious and averse to changing the status quo.

The first challenge for a salesperson is to understand who your enemies are within your accounts. Anti-champions are often difficult to spot. Sometimes, those who have the greatest opposition to you and your solutions will sit quietly through your presentation and ask limited questions, just to point out a weakness here and there. They lie low until the decision is being discussed behind closed doors and then lobby for their own political agenda.

The best way to uncover potential anti-champions is to network within the account. Ask around. It's a mistake to poll only those people who support your solution. In fact, you can learn a lot about your accounts by asking questions like, "Does anyone in your company have concerns about our proposal?" Or, "Who on the decision committee do you think will be least excited about our solution?"

After you identify potential anti-champions within your accounts, you must have a strategy for dealing with them so they don't undermine your efforts. This is something that has puzzled the selling establishment for decades. The traditional approach for dealing with anti-champions has always been for salespeople to stand up to their opponents and attempt to turn them around. The problem is, it's rare that you will ever turn an anti-champion around by standing toe-to-toe with them. Sure, sellers can argue their points. But most anti-champions don't want to hear your arguments. That's why they're called anti-champions. Even if they do listen to what you have to say, it's unlikely that they will change their position. As my grandfather (Derps) used to say, "Just because you shut me up, doesn't mean you've changed my mind."

If you want better results, then I would recommend against trying to defeat the anti-champions within your accounts. These battles are difficult to win, particularly if the opposing person has some influence over the final decision. Instead, your best bet is to neutralize your anti-champions. Rather than trying to convince anti-champions that your product or service is better than their preferred alternative, you would be much better off aiming your arrows at a different target.

My goal in dealing with anti-champions is simple—I try to get them to agree that more than one solution would address their needs. I am willing to concede that they may have reasons for favoring their alternative solution over mine, but I want them to agree that either product would do the job. Knowing that the typical anti-champion starts with the position that their solution is far superior to yours, if you can reach a middle ground by agreeing that either solution would accomplish the objective, you have made significant progress in the sale. You have turned an active opponent into a neutral influence. Of course, once you succeed in neutralizing your anti-champions, you should then work with your own internal champions to create momentum that will sway the decision in your favor.

Lesson 64
Qualify Early, But Not Too Early

It is important to qualify new prospect opportunities. Salespeople should not waste time chasing bad business or expend valuable selling resources with opportunities that will not turn into mutually beneficial sales transactions. Be careful though, because there is also a risk that comes with qualifying too early.

When I sold for NetFrame, if I had gone out into my respective territory looking for prospects that were already budgeted to buy superservers, I would not have sold many systems. Superservers were a new technology. And as with most missionary sales, our best prospects were companies that did not yet know they needed a superserver. The same is true when selling insurance. If a life insurance salesperson, for example, only targets prospects that are already planning to buy life insurance in the coming year, they will probably starve. Most people don't think about buying life insurance until they sit down with a competent insurance professional who will help build a plan that will protect their family from financial distress in the event of an untimely death or disability.

Qualifying too early can cause salespeople to miss out on a pool of prospects they didn't expect. In many instances, sellers must help prospects recognize the need. Of course, sellers should also work to expand the need by uncovering multiple implications, in order to create a broader opportunity to provide value within their target accounts.

> Besides qualifying too early, there is also a risk in qualifying too harshly

Besides qualifying too early, there is also a risk in qualifying too harshly. Potential buyers are easily offended when salespeople take the overly aggressive approach of asking, "Mr. Prospect, am I wasting my time with this account?" A variation of this could sound like, "Mr. Prospect, I don't want to waste your time or mine." Both of these communicate a message that is too self-serving for my taste. Your prospect could easily conclude, "If helping me work through my needs is a waste of your time, then don't bother. I can find someone else who is willing to invest time with me."

Lesson 65
Flatten Your Hockey Stick

One of the challenges facing many sales organizations is the hockey stick pattern that develops as sales spike upwards at

The "Hockey Stick" Phenomenon

Quarterly Sales

Month 1   Month 2   Month 3

the end of each fiscal quarter. This phenomenon occurs in response to the pressures of Wall Street, which drives companies and salespeople to pull in every piece of business they can to meet quarterly sales goals. As a result, lucrative discounts are dangled in front of prospective customers in an effort to entice them to move forward with a purchase. Of course, after quarter-end passes and the special discounts go away, sales slow down again until a similar spike in revenue reoccurs at the end of the following quarter.

End-of-quarter spikes in sales pose significant challenges for the revenue side of a business. They jeopardize the accuracy of the forecast and increase the risk of missing the company's sales projection. A quarterly spike in revenue is also problematic for the operations side of the business. To stay ahead of demand, companies need to be able to accurately predict how much product to manufacture or risk potential delivery problems when the sales backlog exceeds production.

While I wanted to achieve my sales goals by the end of each quarter, my employer wanted us to flatten this hockey stick pattern. Management also wanted the revenue, but they did not want the sales organization to wait until the end of the quarter to close business. Therefore, in an attempt to achieve consistency throughout the quarter, I stopped trying to entice potential buyers with quarter-end discounts and instead changed my approach.

Before we get too deep into a strategy discussion, let's dispel the myth that end-of-quarter sales are made at the end of a quarter. Particularly in larger sales, if a customer is not already working toward a purchase transaction by the end of the quarter, it's unlikely that any last-ditch effort on your part will close a sale that is not ready to be closed. To give yourself a legitimate opportunity to wrap a sale up by the end of a quarter, the closing process should start three to six weeks before the quarter actually ends.

> If the customer is not already working toward a purchase transaction by the end of a quarter, it's unlikely that any last-ditch effort on your part will close a sale that is not ready to be closed.

Here's what I do. For deals that have a legitimate chance of closing by the end of a fiscal quarter, I approach the customer (in advance) and say, "Mr. Prospect, we are very interested in earning your business. But since Wall Street closely watches our company, we would also like to meet or exceed analyst's expectations for the quarter. Therefore, we would much rather consummate a sales transaction on March 31st, than April 1st. We don't want to push you into anything, but we would like to offer an additional discount or incentive that might make a March transaction mutually beneficial. The question is, does it make sense for us to have a conversation about the possibility of wrapping this sale up in March?"

This positioning will intrigue most customers enough to

ask, "What's the incentive?" Although theirs is a legitimate question, now is not the time to get into specifics about your special offer. The objective here is not to propose a discount, at least not yet. You are simply conveying that your company is interested in pulling business into the current quarter and you want to know if it makes sense to pursue a more in-depth discussion. If they indicate that an end-of-quarter transaction is indeed possible, then I set up a meeting where we can sit down and discuss possible incentives. If they want you to tell them what the incentive is up-front, say, "I don't know because I haven't yet gone to management on your behalf. At this point, I just wanted to see if you were close enough to a decision to warrant the conversation." If your prospect is close to a decision, they will want to know more about your offer. This creates a window of opportunity for you to package and propose a special incentive that will make a March transaction mutually beneficial.

Talk Dollar Discounts, Not Percentages

When offering special incentives, I encourage salespeople to stay away from percentage discounts. Percentages are usually non impactful. So many companies out there are offering such steep discounts (all the way up to 70% off), that if you are not prepared to offer an additional 30%, 40%, or 50% off your proposed price, your percentage discount will likely sound small and insignificant to someone who is constantly hearing about larger discounts.

I never talk percentage discounts. Instead, I put any special incentives I plan to offer in hard dollar terms. This gives your discounts more teeth by making them sound like better incentives. When I want to wrap up a quarter-end deal, for example, I might say, "Mr. Prospect, when we last talked, I asked if it would make sense to offer you a special incentive to move forward with a decision this quarter." With my revised quote in hand, I would then add, "If you are ready to move forward with a purchase, we would be willing to discount your cost by an additional $4,500. Essentially, it's worth $4,500 for us to book your order on March 31st, as opposed to April 1st."

I also say the following as a disclaimer. "Mr. Prospect, this incentive is not intended to pressure you in any way. We merely want to offer those customers who are ready to make a decision an incentive to pull the trigger one day sooner." Taking the pressure off with a softer approach is almost always more productive. We will talk more about this later.

My positioning also protects against having prospects come back next month asking for the same special discount. This happens a lot to sellers in the corporate environment who just slash their price and hope. Offering a specific discount for a specific reason, however, puts you in a strong position to explain to prospects that the discount was offered as an incentive to book the business within a given timeframe (i.e. March), and there is unfortunately no way to go backward in time.

You Can Also Pull Deals into Months One and Two

After offering special incentives, sellers who wrap their deals up by the end of the quarter are often left with a skimpy forecast. Of course, buyers have learned to hold off another three months knowing that the best deals won't come until the end of next quarter. As a result of this built-in buying cycle, the familiar hockey stick pattern becomes a self-fulfilling prophecy. Fortunately for sellers, the same strategy we used for closing deals at quarter-end can also be used to pull deals up into the first two months of the current quarter.

For those customers who were not ready to have a conversation about moving forward with a purchase at the end of last quarter, don't offer a special incentive at the end of the quarter. Why bother if they're not ready? Instead, I wait until the deal begins to ripen, say on April 17th. At that point, I approach the prospect saying, "We are very interested in earning your business. But one thing my company is trying to prevent is the traditional hockey stick spike in revenue that occurs at the end of every fiscal quarter. Essentially, we would like to pull deals forward in the quarter—into months one and two. Therefore, we would like to see if it makes sense to offer a mutual incentive to consummate this sale earlier in the quarter rather than waiting until the end of June?"

I recommend against offering customers a special incentive in December, and then if they don't move forward with a purchase, showing up with another incentive in January. I addressed this earlier by making the point that I only offer special incentives if there is a legitimate chance that the sale will close within the targeted timeframe.

The hidden beauty of this technique is that it gives salespeople many more milestones for closing sales. Most of your competitors (until they read this book) will only be offering special deals four times per year—at the end of each quarter. You, on the other hand, can craft all kinds of scenarios that will accelerate your customer's timeframe and satisfy your objectives for pulling revenue forward.

Lesson 66
Is Cost Justification Your Friend?

Cost justification is one of the hurdles that every salesperson must clear on the way to completing a successful sales transaction. If the company you represent sells valuable products and services, you will ultimately have to be able to cost-justify your proposal. More importantly, prospective buyers will have to cost-justify the purchase to their management.

Those sales where prospects have a pressing need are relatively easy to cost-justify, so let's not spend a lot of time talking about them. Instead, let's focus on those opportunities where the prospect is trying to decide if the value of your solution is worth its cost. With most customers, this assessment will likely determine whether or not you succeed in making a sale.

Cost justification starts with needs development. If a customer doesn't perceive a need, then by definition, they won't find value in the solutions you offer. Conversely, customers who recognize greater needs have more reasons to buy, and that makes your job significantly easier. We want potential buyers to recognize needs, and we also want them to recognize our value as we proceed through the sales process. That's why we spent so much time talking about needs development in *Secrets of Question Based Selling*. But as the end of a sale draws closer, prospects must be able to weigh their options and make educated decisions about which solutions are most cost-effective. That's where your approach to justification, as the salesperson on the account, plays an important role in your success in making a sale.

Here are three strategies that will help you work with customers to cost justify more decisions in your favor.

Always Compare Apples to Apples

When I sold NetFrame superservers, a large configuration of our mainframe-style product could cost well over $100,000. This price was often being compared to low-end PC-based products at only a fraction of the price. As a result, customers would ask us, "How can we justify spending $100,000 on a NetFrame when we can buy a Compaq Proliant for $40,000?"

Without any justification, customers could conclude that they would save $60,000 by purchasing a Compaq over a NetFrame. But this was not an apples to apples comparison. NetFrame offered so much more capacity than traditional PC servers, that in reality, a NetFrame superserver could be the functional equivalent of five (or eight) Compaq machines. Therefore, when customers realized that their decision was to either buy one NetFrame, or as many as eight PC servers (at $40,000 each), NetFrame quickly became the more cost-effective solution, in addition to having many other desirable features.

Don't Let Customers Strip Away Your Differentiation

We must remember that customers are negotiating too. And one of the common negotiating ploys customers use is to try and strip away a vendor's differentiation in order to get a lower price. Customers will say, "Why should I pay $100,000 for your solution (as in the previous example) when your competitor offers a similar product for much less money?"

If you are trying to sell a commodity product for a premium price, you will lose every sale. Customers can't justify spending more when they can get the same product somewhere else for less. But if the products and services you offer truly are different, you cannot let customers strip away your differentiation during the negotiation.

I used to offer my customers a tongue-in-cheek dose of perspective by saying, "Mr. Prospect, you can absolutely purchase a PC server for $40,000. You could buy a new Volkswagen for $25,000. You could also buy a piano for $10,000. But none of these offer the same performance or functional capabilities as a NetFrame."

> Purchasing a lower-priced alternative that doesn't accomplish the prospect's objectives will not save them money.

The goal here is not to be sarcastic or flippant. If all things were equal, your solution would be commoditized, and customers would always gravitate to the lower-priced alternative. But in high-value strategic sales, all things are not always equal. Therefore, let's make it easy. If a prospect does not want or need what your product delivers, they should *not* buy it. If, however, the prospect does need what your product or service offers, then purchasing a lower-priced alternative that doesn't accomplish their objectives will not save them money. It is your responsibility as their salesperson to point this out.

Smaller Pieces are Easier to Cost Justify

When Laura and I first started shopping for a house in Atlanta, we had a definite budget in mind. Our financial situation at the time dictated that we could spend up to $180,000. Sure enough, we found the perfect house, and as you might guess, it had a price tag of $225,000, which exceeded our intended price range. To both of us, $225,000 seemed too much to spend for a house.

Jerry Saunders, our real estate agent, saw things differently. Instead of trying to justify the $225,000 price that was beyond our reach, Jerry focused on justifying the differential. He reasoned that after negotiating a deal with the seller, we could probably get the house for as little as $205,000, which was only $25,000 higher than our original price target. Jerry also pointed out that this house had just been painted (a $5,000 value), the extended warranty on the home was still active (a $3,500 value), and it had a termite contract (another $2,000 value). Now the difference in value was only $14,500. After these considerations, the difference in cost was much easier to swallow, and we went ahead with the purchase.

Sometimes it is much easier to justify smaller pieces of a bigger decision, than to bite off the whole shebang. Once Jerry broke the decision down, we started to see the cost-benefit of each component. We were already comfortable with the idea of spending $180,000. All Jerry had to do was make us comfortable enough to justify the differential in cost.

Transform Your Benefits into Hard Dollars

One of the most productive cost-justification strategies is to transform the benefits you offer into hard-dollar savings. For example, if your product or service is capable of increasing the customer's productivity by 30% to 50% over the next five years, how much money does that represent? If you provide a solution that would reduce the customer's cost of maintenance, eliminate downtime, or reduce overhead, you would strengthen your case by estimating these benefits in dollar terms, to show customers how purchasing your product or service would improve their existing condition.

Transforming benefits into hard-dollar projections is a key component of many successful sales. When potential buyers realize that spending money on your solution will make them financially better off, it becomes much easier for them to pull the trigger on a purchase.

What's the Cost of Not Buying Your Product?

Sellers focus most of their cost-justification efforts trying to point out how their solutions will add value. Essentially, the traditional justification argument has always been to show prospects that they will be much better off if they go ahead and purchase your proposed solution.

There is an opportunity to take the opposite position, however. Rather than just reiterating your value proposition, what if you focused on the cost of *not* buying your product or service? This makes a powerful justification argument, because choosing *not* to purchase your product or service could be the customer's most expensive alternative.

To illustrate, several years ago I solicited price estimates from several roofing contractors to repair some shingles that had deteriorated on our roof. Initial price estimates were higher than expected, ranging between $2,500 and $3,500 to fix the problem. Not surprisingly, I put the decision off until later. A few weeks passed and I received a note from one of the contractors who bid on the project. He had invested the time to prepare a second quote, showing how much it would cost to repair my roof a year from now—approximately $8,500. Needless to say, the higher cost of his second quote got my attention. A year from now, his quote explained, rather than just needing a few shingles replaced, I would be facing the possibility of having to replace the entire roof. Essentially, by pointing out that waiting could make my current problems significantly worse, he created a sense of urgency that ultimately caused me to hire his company to come over and repair our roof.

So, what's the cost of *not* buying the service contract on a large piece of manufacturing equipment, and then being without support when something goes wrong? What's the cost of *not* buying life insurance, and then being unable to protect your family in the event that something unexpected happens to you? How much does it cost if a company chooses *not* to upgrade their technology platform, and as a result, is gobbled up by a competitor?

Valuable solutions do require a financial investment on the part of the buyer, but in many cases, the consequences of *not* buying a product or service can far outweigh the actual expenditure. Once again, you should make it your responsibility (as a sales professional) to point out that the cost of *not* buying your solution may be the customer's most expensive option.

Summary Point

Particularly for customers who are very concerned about cost, it should be pointed out that another very expensive way to buy your product or service is to buy the wrong solution first, before buying the right one. One has to wonder how many times buyers have skimped to save a few dollars, only to discover that the promise offered by the lowest priced alternative did not fulfill their needs or meet their expectations.

Lesson 67
Don't be Defensive on Price

For many sellers, price is a villainous obstacle that gets in the way of prospects pulling the trigger on a favorable decision. It is the one objection that is guaranteed to come up at some point in every sale. Every salesperson, at some point in their careers, has lost a sale (or will lose one) because of a pricing issue. Pricing also causes prospects to hesitate before purchasing, to reexamine their alternatives or look more closely at your competitors. As a result, it's not surprising that sellers tend to be defensive when it comes to price.

> Whenever a salesperson sounds tentative or defensive about their price, prospects are quick to assume that negotiations are not yet over.

To make matters worse, whenever a salesperson sounds even the least bit tentative or defensive about their price, prospects are quick to assume that price negotiations are not yet over. They will assume that you are hiding something—additional discounts or better contract terms. As sellers, this is the last thing we want—to have our own lack of confidence (about the price we charge) turn into a possible integrity problem in the eyes of our customers.

Here's the good news. Sellers don't have to be defensive about price. If this issue is positioned correctly in the sale, then the price of your product or service should be your friend, not your enemy. But just like anything, this may require a proactive effort on your part to re-think how you are currently positioning price, and how you could more positively impact the outcome of your sales. Consider the following:

Buyers Don't Always Choose the Lowest Price

When I speak to sales audiences, I often broach this issue by saying, "Can you please raise your hand if you drive the least expensive car?" Usually, very few hands get raised. Then, I ask, "How many people in this audience wear the cheapest clothes, live in the lowest-cost housing, or eat whatever is most economical?" The answer is, nobody does. Then why do salespeople spend so much time worrying that they aren't going to win because they don't offer the lowest-priced alternative?

Customers are just like us in the sense that they rarely buy the least expensive product. Take a look at your existing customer base. I bet very few of your customers hire the lowest-wage employees, buy the cheapest computer systems, or occupy the least expensive office space. Likewise, if you examine the largest companies in the world, you will find that very few are successful because they sell the lowest-priced products. No one has ever accused IBM of having the lowest price—or General Electric, SAP, Westinghouse, American Air Lines, Lockheed Martin, Microsoft, Nortel Networks, Pfizer, or Merrill Lynch. None of these companies hangs its hat on offering the cheapest solutions; yet they are all perennial sales leaders in their respective industries. It's because people usually don't buy products or services just because they are lowest in price.

Decisions are Based on Value, Not Price

If customers are not buying the lowest-priced product, then what *are* they buying? The answer is clear. They're buying those products and services that offer the greatest value—in other words, the most bang for the buck.

> Price becomes the dominant issue if and when your product or service gets commoditized.

For buyers, the concepts of price and value are going to be one and the same. To increase the value of the proposed product or service, they want the seller to reduce their price. From the seller's perspective, however, there are two ways to increase your value proposition. One is to lower your price. The other option is to raise the perceived value of your proposed solution.

Price becomes the dominant issue if and when your product or service gets commoditized. When a prospective buyer believes they can get the same features, benefits, quality, and support from more than one source, they make decisions based on who offers the lowest price. When everything else is equal, decisions will always come down to price. Therefore, it's your job as a sales professional to make sure everything is not equal. That means causing prospects to recognize that your solutions offer more features, promise greater benefits, are higher in quality, and come with better support.

At the end of the day, those sellers who have succeeded in

increasing the perceived value of their products and services will outsell their counterparts who try to influence the outcome of the sale just by reducing their price.

What's the Number One Reason People Buy From You?

Why do customers buy from you? When I ask this question, salespeople and sales managers are quick to respond with things like, "People buy from us because of our state-of-the-art products," or, "We are industry leaders." While these things may be true, neither is the main reason people buy from you.

> The number one reason customers buy from you is because you offer the most cost-effective solutions that will achieve their desired result.

Ironically, the number one reason customers buy from you is cost. For someone to make a buying decision, they must conclude that your product or service is the least expensive alternative that provides the features, benefits, qualities, and overall solution they want. Being the lowest-cost alternative does not mean having the lowest price, however. When I purchased my first BMW, I obviously wasn't looking for the least expensive automobile. But my desire to own a nice car didn't negate my need for value. After investigating numerous options, I chose the BMW because it was the most cost-effective alternative that provided the features and benefits I wanted. That's why customers buy from you too—because you, your company, and your solutions offer the most cost-effective solutions that will achieve their desired result.

I make this point because if we recognize that the number

one reason customers buy from us is cost effectiveness, we reduce our risk of sounding defensive on price. Personally, I go on the offensive when it comes to price. In my current business, I tell customers, "If you want the cheapest sales training, Question Based Selling is not for you." Frankly, most people know that you only get what you pay for anyway. I quickly add, "If, on the other hand, you want to bring in strategic sales methodology that will significantly increase the effectiveness and productivity of your entire sales team, that's what Question Based Selling delivers."

Be Careful Who You Turn to for Advice

One of my clients recently asked me to deliver the keynote address at their National Sales Meeting in San Mateo. The evening prior, I was invited to attend their awards dinner. Following dinner, the Vice President of Sales took the stage to honor the company's top performers from the previous fiscal year. He recognized each person individually by sharing little anecdotes as these top guns came up to the stage (amid rousing rounds of applause) to be recognized for their outstanding performance.

I focused on the faces of these top-performing salespeople as they paraded by. To me, there's nothing more crisp and sure than the expression of a confident salesperson who has achieved the highest level of excellence in their profession.

The next morning, it was my turn to take the stage, and I must admit, I was in rare form that day as I delivered a powerful message about the challenges salespeople face in today's increasingly competitive marketplace. I too received a very appreciative round of applause from the audience.

After a short break, the next event on the meeting agenda was a panel discussion intended to provide a company-wide forum where people could ask questions or share concerns with the executive staff. I was invited to sit on the panel as an objective third party opinion. The very first issue that came up was price. Apparently, some people in the sales organization were aggressively lobbying to lower the price in order to remain competitive. In their eyes, deals were being lost because the price of the product was too high. Other salespeople argued that the product was very marketable at current price levels and they were adamant about *not* changing it. The marketing department was caught in the middle. They didn't know whom to believe. After several minutes of lively debate, one of the marketing people turned to me and asked, "Tom, you're the expert, what do you think?" Suddenly, I was caught in the middle, knowing that taking either side of this argument was likely to produce a certain amount of animosity.

"Let's poll the audience," I said. "Could I ask everyone who was recognized at last night's performance dinner (as a top producer) to please raise your hands." Many hands in the audience went up. "Now," I continued, "can I ask that you please keep your hands raised if you agree that the price of your products and services is too high and should be reduced." Guess what? Every hand that was raised instantly came down. A quiet laughter broke out among the audience. Suddenly, the message was clear. For top performers, price was a non-issue. Those salespeople who were struggling, however, were blaming the price for their lack of success.

There is an important lesson to be learned from this story. Some fraction of the sales organization in every company will complain about price. In their minds, price is the reason they are losing sales. What they want is to be able to offer more benefits than their competitors at a lower price. While that is a noble goal, companies that offer the best product typically don't have the absolute lowest price. That's why companies need salespeople—to differentiate their respective companies and the value of their proposed solutions.

Therefore, we must ponder the question: whose advice should we be listening to—top performers who believe that price is not an issue, or salespeople who are struggling, and consistently losing deals because of price?

Lesson 68
Range Pricing

At some point in the sales process, usually after you've had an opportunity to present your product or service, it is time to submit a proposal. Your proposal should answer the question, "What is your recommended solution, and how much does it cost?" Your proposal gives prospective buyers the information they need to compare your solution against other alternatives.

For many of us, delivering a proposal represents the ultimate moment of truth in the sale. If the perceived value of your product or service is greater than its proposed cost, then justifying a purchase will be relatively easy. If, however, the cost of a recommended solution exceeds its perceived value, the prospect's enthusiasm will be replaced by a sense of indifference, and your probability of making a sale will be significantly reduced.

The proposal process has become a high-risk event for many salespeople because it is often veiled in secrecy. In today's business environment, sellers have been conditioned to hold something back for negotiations, and buyers have been conditioned that sellers are usually holding something back. To me, this fosters a certain "us against them" mentality which can be counterproductive to building mutually beneficial business relationships.

When I deliver a proposal, I would rather sound helpful and open than cautious or reluctant. Likewise, I would rather continue working in partnership with my prospects than take a position on the opposite side of the negotiating table. While I do agree with the adage that it's smart to leave some "meat on the bone" for closing the sale, I cannot side with the notion that proposals should be shrouded in secrecy.

Here's an example of what I mean. Joe Salesperson arrives early for his two o'clock appointment with Craig Johnson, the CFO for ABC Company, a lucrative prospect in Joe's territory. ABC Company is evaluating new telephony systems and Craig liked what he saw during Joe's initial presentation last Thursday. As a result, he asked Joe to put together a formal proposal for ABC Company.

Since then, Joe has worked hard to respond to Mr. Johnson's request. After working through the numbers multiple times, Joe has put together a proposal that he hopes will be financially attractive to his customer and well positioned against other competing vendors, while still maintaining a reasonable profit margin and a lucrative commission opportunity.

Two o'clock rolls around and it's now the moment of truth for Joe. He exchanges pleasantries with Mr. Johnson and as they get down to business, Joe reaches into a large briefcase on the floor. After shuffling through some papers and catalogues, Joe pulls out a manila folder marked, "ABC Company." Foraging through the manila folder, which is packed with various documents, Joe carefully extracts what appears to be a proposal. Joe then stuffs everything else back into his folder, and returns the folder to its original position in his briefcase on the floor. Finally, Joe looks up and is ready to discuss *his proposal.*

> Do you think prospects believe that most salespeople practice full disclosure when they deliver proposals?

Do you think prospects believe that most salespeople practice full disclosure when they deliver proposals? The answer is a resounding no. As I said earlier, buyers have been conditioned that salespeople are usually holding something back. In this case, if I were the prospect, I would be wondering what else might be in Joe's manila envelope (or in his briefcase) that I didn't get to see. My skepticism would cause me to push Joe for more information, to make sure I was getting the best deal.

Do you really want to provoke your prospects to feel that they have to push for the truth, the whole truth, and nothing but the truth? Of course not. That puts you in a very defensive position in the sale. We said earlier that it was important not to be defensive on price. Let's not be defensive when it comes to delivering proposals either. That's why I recommend a proactive strategy we call *range pricing.* This technique of range pricing is one of the most productive, open, and down-to-earth strategies you can use when delivering proposals. Let me show you how it works.

What Makes the Home Depot Special?

In 1978, Bernie Marcus and Arthur Blank co-founded The Home Depot in Atlanta as a warehouse-shopping concept targeting home improvements and the building materials industry. The Home Depot has since expanded into a multi-billion dollar, worldwide business phenomenon that has become one of the greatest retail success stories in history.

But why is The Home Depot so incredibly successful? Sure, they have good prices and friendly service. But lots of stores have good prices and friendly service people. The real question is: what is it that compels customers to enter a Home Depot store looking for a simple roll of tape, and come out with $458.00 worth of power tools and garden supplies? Perhaps the answer to this question can be found in your own experience with retail shopping.

It's a Magical, Mystical Place

Have you ever been shopping in a retail store and found an item that you really liked, but you couldn't find one in your size? If you're like me, you asked the clerk, "Do you happen to have my size in the back?" The clerk said, "I'll check," and then scampered through the curtains or the double doors into a place that we know only as "the back." Several minutes later, the clerk returned through the curtains or double doors with the item you wanted, in your size, and everyone was happy.

What is this magical, mystical place that retailers call *the back*? Apparently, it's a place that contains a secret inventory of all kinds of wonderful things that are in your size. Yet for some reason, customers are not allowed to go back there. I assume that's because it's a magical, mystical place.

Hence the magic of a Home Depot store. As one of the early adopters of the warehouse shopping concept, Bernie Marcus and Arthur Blank were able to create a different type of shopping experience by realizing that when a customer walks through the front doors of a Home Depot, they are automatically in *the back*. The configuration of each Home Depot store provides customers with a virtual warehouse full of home improvement options. As a result, this warehousing concept gives the Home Depot a unique opportunity to bond with its customers, which has enabled them to grow their sales results exponentially.

Invite Your Prospects Into "The Back"

The idea behind range pricing is simple. As a salesperson, I wanted to give prospects more options, rather than fewer. I also wanted potential buyers to feel that I was being open and forthright, rather than give them a reason to be skeptical. And, of course, I wanted to focus the customer's attention on the value of my product, rather than just badgering me for additional discounts.

How does this concept of range pricing work? Let's begin by making a few assumptions. First, most salespeople are able to craft their proposals(s) from an array of different solutions options, depending on what the customer needs. Therefore, whether you sell medical equipment, financial services, office supplies, or technology, it is assumed that you will tailor your proposals based on any number of variables including volume, contract terms, configuration options, special financing, implementation timeframe, and so on.

The next assumption we need to make is that most prospects don't buy the first proposal that gets put in front of them. Especially with larger decisions, potential buyers want to participate in evaluating the best alternatives and they want to negotiate the final purchase. (Did you buy the very first car you laid eyes on—at list price? Of course, you didn't. I didn't either.)

As we said earlier, very few buyers will choose the low price alternative. Few prospects will choose the highest-priced option either. Most will weigh their options and choose one that is somewhere in the middle. A range pricing strategy is, therefore, designed to give prospects multiple decision alternatives by giving them a range of proposal options. Essentially, you make the proposal process easy by inviting prospects into *the back* and giving them multiple options from which to choose.

Create a Range of Proposal Options

I spent the last five years of my corporate career selling superserver technology. NetFrame designed and manufactured high-end computer platforms that were able to consolidate large corporate networks onto a single superserver. Depending on customer needs, these machines ranged in price from a base unit that might cost as little as $19,000, all the way up to a large enterprise platform with a price tag exceeding $300,000.

After preparing a few proposals, I got pretty good at knowing which superserver model and configuration would best suit the customer's needs. But if I tried to present *what I thought* was the perfect configuration, my prospects always seemed to want something different. People have a very difficult time accepting someone else's opinion, and they probably won't buy into the very first idea that comes along anyway. That's why I started delivering a range of separate proposal options.

Knowing that most buyers want choices, I started experimenting with the idea of giving prospects an opportunity to choose between multiple different proposal options, as opposed to trying to deliver the perfect solution by presenting a single proposal. I remember my first experiment vividly. The prospect needed a superserver that would have cost approximately $80,000, but I went ahead and created five separate proposals that ranged in price from an entry unit that cost approximately $20,000, all the way up to an enterprise machine that priced out at $120,000. Essentially, I followed The Home Depot's model by giving my customer more information rather than less, which allowed them to choose between several different options.

There is no magic in the number five. You can provide four proposal options and still accomplish the same objective. Personally, I like to offer five separate proposals because most prospects immediately discard the highest option and the lowest, which enabled us to focus on the three remaining proposals to work toward solidifying a deal.

Your Extra Effort Builds Credibility

Offering a range of pricing alternatives puts a salesperson in a unique position of strength. By giving prospects multiple proposal options, you have an opportunity to be proactive by saying:

Salesperson: "Mr. Prospect, you asked me to create a proposal that would reflect your environment. But, rather than coming to you with a single option, I prepared several proposals—to give you a range of configuration alternatives. This will give you an opportunity to choose the proposal option that best serves your business."

Providing a range of different proposal options communicates that you are willing to go above and beyond the call of duty, which is an excellent way to establish credibility and set yourself apart from your competitors. Going above and beyond in the proposal process also demonstrates a commitment to excellence, which is an indication to the customer that you will provide high levels of service after the sale.

A Range Pricing Strategy Can Also Uncover the Budget

Once you prepare a range of proposal options, the next step is to review them with your prospect starting with the smallest first. Take time to explain each of the individual line items on the proposal, including sample configurations and related service options. Be sure to point out any assumptions you made, along with any calculations and how they were derived. And if you haven't already thought of it, reviewing multiple proposal options gives you multiple opportunities to reinforce your value proposition. Service after the sale is very important, but so is service during the sale.

At NetFrame, the smallest proposal I provided was usually an entry-level configuration, one that might cost a mere

$21,450. I would explain that this configuration did not meet the customer's stated requirements, but I wanted to show them an entry-level configuration so they could see how our family of products scaled. After I explained the basic format and the details of the first proposal, I carefully laid it on the conference table and pulled out the next proposal in the range.

The next option might be for a larger NetFrame system that costs $48,320. I would explain the details of the second config- uration and let the prospect know that although this pro- posal was more robust, it still

> Service after the sale is very important, but so is service during the sale.

didn't have some of the components and capabilities they would probably need. Then, I carefully laid the second pro- posal on the table next to the first, and introduced the third option. "This proposal, Mr. Prospect," I would interject, "more closely matches the specifications for your upcoming project." Of course, proposal number three would be higher in price, perhaps $72,880. Can you see a pattern developing here? The fourth and fifth proposals might be for $93,210 and $117,400, respectively. I would position these as follows: "Mr. Prospect, in addition to giving you a proposal that most closely matches your needs, I also wanted to show you what the con- figuration would look like if you choose to expand your project, now, or in the future."

At this point in the discussion, all five proposals would be neatly laid out on the table in front of the prospect. They would invariably reach out with their hand and pick up one of these proposals to examine it more closely, presumably the one in which they have the most interest. If you are patient, the prospect will reach out with their other hand and pick up a second proposal. Ninety-nine times out of a hundred, prospects will gravitate to the two proposals that most closely match their budget. This provided me with a pretty good idea of how much money they expected to spend, which makes it easier to work with prospects to customize a solution that fits both their needs and their budget.

Negotiations Are Not Just About Price

The hidden beauty of this range pricing strategy is that it positions you for a more productive negotiation. As I said earlier, the traditional approach to delivering pricing is to prepare and deliver a single proposal option that you think most closely meets the prospect's needs. But buyers in today's selling environment are skeptical, and few prospects will buy the very first proposal they see. They have been conditioned to believe that the best deals are not in the first proposal. Furthermore, if you provide limited options, prospects focus all their energy on trying to get you to come down in price.

> Few prospects will buy the very first proposal they see. They have been conditioned to believe that the best deals are not in the first proposal.

Contrary to popular opinion, negotiating a sales transaction is not just about price. If a vendor cannot deliver on time or fails to meet the customer's requirements, it doesn't matter how inexpensive their product is. On the other hand, if the customer feels your product is significantly overpriced, it doesn't matter how many benefits you include. To maximize your value proposition, your negotiations should include everything from contract terms, to financing, delivery, availability, service, support, training, and potential future purchases, in addition to price.

By laying out a range of separate proposal options, there are now two ways to adjust the price. Sure, prospects will still lobby for discounts. But this strategy of giving more information rather than less empowers your prospects to change their own price point by adding or removing various components as presented in the different proposal options. You are essentially inviting potential customers to participate in their own success by giving them the opportunity to peek behind the curtain of secrecy that usually accompanies the proposal process. Your reward will be that prospects feel comfortable with the openness of your approach, and therefore are more inclined to buy from you.

Sometimes the Best Defense is a Good Offense

This strategy of providing multiple proposal options is particularly useful if you happen to be engaged in a competitive dogfight against one of your arch-rival competitors. Considering that salespeople are generally defensive when it comes to price, a range pricing strategy gives you a wonderful opportunity to go on the offensive. For example, after unveiling a range of different proposal options, I say: "Mr. Prospect, I don't know how our competitors do business, but we would rather give you multiple proposal options and let you choose, than be secretive or covert about our pricing and force you to guess at how best to proceed."

This positioning lays a nice competitive land mine for your adversaries in the account. Now, if your competitor delivers a single proposal with limited options (like most will), it's likely that prospects will feel more comfortable with the way you deal with potential buyers. After all, people buy from people, and giving prospects a glimpse of what's *in the back* can go a long way toward making them feel comfortable enough to move forward with a purchase.

> "Mr. Prospect, we would rather give you multiple proposal options and let you choose, than be secretive or covert about our pricing and force you to guess at how best to proceed."

Summary Point

Skeptics usually don't make favorable buying decisions. One way you can make buyers less skeptical is to be forthright with information rather than coy or reserved. This is particularly important when it comes to price because that's where potential buyers tend to focus much of their concern.

For some, creating multiple proposals may sound like extra work. But I assure you, it's not. To me, extra work comes from all the hoops you will have to jump through when prospects believe they have to push you to understand their options and ultimately get the best deal. In today's computer age, proposal boilerplates can be easily manipulated to make the task of creating multiple proposal options relatively simple. You will probably have to tailor your proposal anyway, so why not be proactive by providing multiple proposal options up front. Your investment will not go unnoticed, and your "extra effort" will be duly rewarded.

Lesson 69
Higher Prices Can Increase Your Perceived Value

When it comes to buying value, let me ask you this question. Would you rather buy a $20,000 Mercedes Benz for $20,000, or a $30,000 Mercedes Benz for $20,000? If you are like most people, you would want the better deal—in this case, buying the more expensive car for $20,000.

When I sold Hospital Information Systems for Baxter, we offered a technologically superior product that carried with it a premium price. In the typical opportunity, our HIS proposal would come in twenty to twenty-five percent higher than some of our competitors. Even though Baxter's system offered significant functional advantages over other solutions, justifying the difference in price was still a challenge.

At quarterly sales meetings, some of Baxter's salespeople complained about the price. Usually it was just a few voices in the crowd, but as you might guess, those who were selling the least usually complained the loudest. Surprisingly, Baxter obliged by announcing an across-the-board twenty percent reduction in list price in our family of products. There was only one catch—no more discounting at the lower price.

As the new pricing was rolled out to the field, it soon became apparent that it was much more difficult to sell $80,000 worth of software for $80,000, than it was to propose a $100,000 system, and offer a discount that would enable us to close the sale at $80,000. Customers don't want to pay list price. That's because they want more bang for their buck. Ironically, the salespeople who had previously complained

229

about the old price had even more trouble justifying the lower price. Luckily, the rest of us, who continued to propose the previous price and offer discounts, were virtually unaffected.

The lesson here is simple. Lowering your price can also lower the perceived value of your product or service. Conversely, quoting higher prices and offering discounts can cause prospective buyers to feel that they are getting a better deal. Case in point: Have you purchased furniture lately? Why do you think every furniture store in America is always having a big sale? It's because buyers want to feel they are getting more value for their money.

Lesson 70
Be the Hero...Not the Goat

$H=R-E$. Although you might not recognize this simple formula, it's one of the metaphysical laws of the universe. Actually, it's a QBS equation we use to characterize the cause and effect relationship that determines how satisfied your customers will be at the conclusion of a sale. In layman's terms, happiness (H) is the difference between expectations (E) and reality (R).

Customer satisfaction is a relatively simple concept. If the product or service being delivered meets or exceeds customer expectations, then you will have a happy customer. If, however, what actually gets delivered falls short of expectations, you can expect to have a customer who is dissatisfied.

When customers are unhappy, salespeople are quick to

blame the delivering mechanism, saying that someone in the company should have been more responsive, or the product should have been more robust. But for many sellers, especially those who find themselves dealing with an unusually high frequency of customer problems, this might be an opportunity to look in the mirror. Oftentimes, the root cause of customer dissatisfaction issues has something to do with the expectations that were set during the sales process. I learned my lesson about this in 1992 when I first started selling computer hardware.

At the time, our manufacturing department could build and deliver a fully configured high-end custom server in ten days—seven days if we really pushed.

> If the product or service being delivered meets or exceeds customer expectations, then you will have a happy customer.

Sure enough, in the first superserver sale I closed, the customer asked, "How soon can we get the machine?"

"Ten days," I replied. "But I can probably get it for you in seven."

On the seventh day, the customer called asking, "What's the status of our superserver order?" To find out, I called our manufacturing division to get a status. Not surprisingly, I got the standard answer. They were "working on it."

On the eighth day, the customer called again, "Where's our machine?"

I tried to reiterate that it takes seven to ten days to build a superserver, but all they remembered was me saying that I could deliver their hardware in seven days. Of course, as the ninth and tenth days passed, the customer got more and more nervous, and less and less happy. When their system arrived twelve days after their original order was placed, the mood on-site at the customer's location office was somber and distrusting. Suddenly, we were dealing with an unhappy customer.

When the customer first asked about delivery, I assumed that I was helping them (and myself) by telling them their machine might arrive early. Instead, the expectations I had set created a customer satisfaction issue when the machine showed up only two days late. Never again, I vowed to myself.

When the next customer asked (as they always did), "When can we expect delivery?" I pointed to the fine print on the paperwork and told them to plan on thirty days. I explained that this lead time would give them an opportunity to prepare their physical plant and plan the implementation.

Changing the customer's expectations didn't change the actual time required to build a superserver. Manufacturing could still deliver a fully configured high-end custom server in approximately ten days. But, the customer's mood was suddenly very different when I called after ten or eleven days saying, "Mr. Customer, I did a little extra work on your behalf and your superserver is now ready." Talk about creating happy customers!

In case you were wondering, some customers couldn't wait 30 days for their hardware, in which case they would ask, "Is there anything you can do to get the computer here sooner?" This request actually provided me with a greater opportunity for customer satisfaction.

"When do you need the machine?" I would ask. If their timeframe was reasonable, I would respond by saying, "Let me see what I can do to expedite your order." Once again, whether their machine showed up on time or early, I was suddenly the hero…not the goat.

It's amazing how many salespeople give potential buyers the best case scenario thinking they are helping the situation, when they are actually setting expectations that cannot be consistently met or exceeded.

Lesson 71
Work Backward to Move Your Sale Forward

One of the things I learned in high school chemistry was the theory of gaseous expansion—the phenomenon that gasses expand naturally to fill the space available. Over the course of my professional selling career, I have realized that a similar phenomenon occurs in sales—decision cycles expand to fill the timeframe alotted. When potential buyers don't feel a sense of urgency to make a decision, they will likely put the decision off until later.

Putting a decision off until later creates an obvious problem for salespeople. Sellers want opportunities to move toward closure, but pushing harder usually causes prospects to start pushing back. Instead of pushing harder, the key to shortening the sales process is to do something that will increase the prospect's sense of urgency for making a decision.

One of the most effective ways to increase your prospect's sense of urgency is to work backward from the projected implementation date. For example, if you were selling telecommunication equipment, you might say, "Mr. Prospect, if I could ask you to think past the purchase decision for a moment, when would you like to have this equipment installed and fully operational in your business?"

This is a very powerful qualifying question. If it appears that your prospect hasn't thought much about their implementation, then they probably aren't close to making a decision. On the other hand, if they are serious about buying your product or service, they will likely have an implementation plan in mind with target dates and project deadlines.

> One of the most effective ways to increase your prospect's sense of urgency is to work backward from the projected implementation date.

Focusing on the timeframe for implementation as opposed to the status of an order is valuable because it allows the salesperson to follow up with the prospect without hounding them for the actual order. Prospects are aware that a salesperson's job is ultimately to close business, but they can only take so much pestering about when the purchase order will be signed.

When you ask about implementation, the prospect might respond by saying, "We would like to have the system operational by January 15th."

If this conversation happens in September, January could seem like a long way off—in which case, it would be a mistake to assume that this prospect will be in a hurry to make a decision. To them, January could sound like sometime next year. Herein lies the value of working backwards from an implementation date. Working backwards gives you an opportunity to increase your prospect's sense of urgency by shortening the time window available to make a decision.

If the customer chooses January 15th as their implementation date, the next question I would ask is, "How much time should we allow for testing before the equipment goes into production?" Very few strategic products are put directly into production on the day they are received. Instead, they are staged, assembled, tested, installed, and then inspected, before being deemed ready for service.

"We should probably allow at least six weeks, two weeks to install the hardware and then thirty days to test our procedures," the prospect might say.

I would continue to work backwards by asking, "Once you have made your decision, how long do you think it will take to get the signatures needed to cut a purchase order?"

"Negotiating the contract might take a couple of weeks, but after that, we could probably cut a PO fairly quickly," the prospect may reply.

The next step is critical. Once you have identified the different elements of the decision process and you understand the lead-times involved, you work backward in the conversation to build a timeline that increases the prospect's sense of urgency for making a decision. For example, I might summarize by saying: "Mr. Prospect, if your system needs to be 'live' January 15th, and we need to allow six weeks for testing, two weeks for staging, and another two weeks for the holidays in December, then we will need to have an order in hand the last week of October to meet your implementation schedule. That means we have approximately thirty days to make a decision."

Suddenly, a project that was going to happen "sometime next year" turns into a decision that needs to be made in the next thirty days. As an added bonus, revising the timeline positions you in more of a customer service role with your prospects. You are essentially helping them plan ahead to make sure their project goes smoothly, which is much more valuable than just pestering them to hurry up and make a decision.

Lesson 72
If You Could Have Everything on Your Wish List

Deals can spiral downward and out of control during negotiations. They can also spiral up. Of course, as salespeople, we want to encourage customers to buy more and not less. But we also want to encourage them to move forward without making them feel pushed or making ourselves sound self-serving. One non-threatening technique you can use to encourage customers to buy more is to have them create a wish list.

In most deals, discounts are based on sales volume. The more you buy, the greater your discount. If you start negotiating from list price, as most sellers do, one of the open questions is volume. How many units does the buyer want to purchase?

Most prospects you negotiate with are limited by a certain budget. But don't be fooled. Budgets are usually more flexible than customers would like us to believe. The trick is to get customers to think beyond their current limitations, whether those limitations are real or perceived. The technique I use is to ask prospects to create a wish list. I say, "Mr. Customer, if cost was not an issue in your decision, and you could have everything on your wish list, how much product would you order?" You could even add a disclaimer, saying, "I'm just playing with numbers here to take advantage of volume." Most prospects will participate in this discussion, because they will want you to "play" with the numbers to see if they can get a better deal.

> Budgets are usually more flexible than customers would like us to believe.

My goal here is to find out how much the prospect might buy if price was not an issue. Customers will rarely buy more than they want. But when the prospect *does* want more, you can now work with them toward finding ways to secure a greater portion of the items on their wish list.

Another idea is to ask, "Mr. Prospect, how many units do you expect to purchase during the next twelve to eighteen months?" By getting prospects to visualize the bigger picture, you can create opportunities to increase the volume of your deals now.

Lesson 73
Negotiate Like a Dentist

You don't need to be defensive on price—we already made this point. Very few people buy a product or service because it has the absolute lowest price. What they buy is value, wanting the biggest bang for their buck. This includes evaluating their solution alternatives and making the best decision.

The challenge for salespeople is getting prospects to compare products in an equitable way. The sale of professional services provides a good example. Why would anyone want to pay in excess of a hundred dollars per hour for a good accountant, when they could have their taxes done at the local H&R Block office for $69.95? Likewise, why would it make sense to pay two or three times as much for an experienced software analyst, when you can hire a bench technician from a local computer outlet for cheap?

> Is it better to pay less money for a less valuable resource, or to pay more for the appropriate level of expertise?

It's especially difficult to quantify benefits with intangibles. From the prospect's point of view, is it better to pay less money for a less valuable resource, or to pay more for a higher level of expertise? Since customers cannot actually see the intangible (in this case, a service) before it's delivered, they often struggle with how to make the best decision. That's why, when QBS clients ask me to help their salespeople justify the premiums they charge for a higher level of expertise, I often suggest that they should try negotiating like a dentist. Here's a cute little parable that illustrates my point.

One day, a dentist was examining a new patient in the chair.

"Hmmm," says the dentist after reviewing the patient's x-rays.

"What's wrong?" asks the patient, sensing the dentist's concern.

"It looks like we need to pull a bum tooth," the dentist answers.

"Oh no!" the patient grimaces. "How much will that cost?"

"About a hundred dollars," the dentist responds.

"How bad will it hurt?" the patient moaned.

"Not bad. It will only take a minute," the dentist replies.

"You're going to charge me a hundred bucks for something that only takes a minute?" the patient challenges.

"Well, how long would you like it to take?" asks the dentist.

To justify the value of your product or service, sometimes it's necessary to change the prospect's perspective. Would you rather pay a little more to have a tooth pulled quickly and painlessly, or risk choosing some other alternative that's less expensive, but comes with a much higher personal cost?

Lesson 74
Ask for More Than You Need

In sales, as in life, people don't always get what they ask for. When prospects, for example, go up the chain of command in their companies to ask for funding on a purchase, they sometimes get a lesser amount than was originally requested. The same thing used to happen to me when I was growing up. I would ask my dad for five dollars (to go to a movie or to the mall) and he would hand me two dollars (three, if he was in a good mood).

Part of qualifying an opportunity is making sure prospects can get the funds necessary to pull the trigger on a purchase.

The lesson here is simple. If one of your prospects needs twenty thousand dollars to purchase your product or service, you should coach your champions in the account to ask for more than they actually need. In this case, they might ask for twenty-five or thirty thousand dollars. Now, if upper management approves a lesser amount, they can still move forward.

> Part of qualifying an opportunity is making sure prospects can get the funds necessary to pull the trigger on a purchase.

Asking for more than you actually need gives you an opportunity to scale back and still accomplish your objective. This is usually much easier than having to go back up the chain of command to ask for more money. If I had only figured this out earlier, perhaps I would have been savvy enough to ask my dad for eight dollars, knowing that it might turn into five.

Lesson 75
What If You Were in My Shoes?

True story. Back in the mid 1980's, when I was selling hospital information systems, I found myself sitting across from a stodgy CFO at a major prospect account. At the time, we were engaged in one of those cat and mouse negotiating sessions, where we both sat there looking at each other wondering who would be the first to crack. The CFO seemed ready to move forward with the purchase, but for some reason, he was being coy and I was running out of closing strategies. Finally, I said, "Mr. Prospect, if you were in my shoes, and you were the salesperson on this account, what would you do?"

He pondered my question for a few seconds (which seemed like an eternity) and gave me a long calculated glaze. Then, the CFO smiled and said, "If I were in your shoes, I would have asked for the order an hour ago." Without a word, I handed over the contract. He burst into laughter and then signed the paperwork. The deal was done. Even though I walked out of the account that day with the order in hand, I wasn't sure if I felt good or bad about it.

What I learned was people love to give advice. They particularly love to pontificate about what they would do if they were in your situation. That's why it's always a good idea to ask, "If our roles were reversed, and you were me, what would you do?" In most sales, your best coach in the account is the person on the other end of the conversation. So, as long as prospects are willing to offer valuable advice, you might as well position yourself to be on the receiving end.

Lesson 76
Silence is Golden

With respect to contract negotiations, there's an old adage that says, "He who talks first loses." There comes a point in every sale where the seller delivers his or her best offer, and the prospect ponders whether or not to move forward. The silence that ensues can be deafening. But, with a little patience on your part, this otherwise awkward moment in the sale can actually become your ally in the decision-making process.

Silence is a useful tool early in the sale. During the needs development process, one of the best things a salesperson can do is ask a question and then shut up. I don't mean to be crass, but if you notice, there is a strong tendency for salespeople to jump in and start talking to fill the silence whenever there is a pause in the conversation. If you refrain and let the customer talk, you will be amazed how much valuable information you can get.

> One of the best things a salesperson can do is ask a question and then shut up.

This same principle about letting customers talk also applies at the negotiating table. Silence has an interesting way of either causing prospects to move forward with a purchase, or smoking out any objections that may stand in the way of a favorable decision. If you want to find out where you stand in the sale, you must resist the temptation to answer your own questions or change the subject in order to fill the silence with noise. Instead, when you ask questions, you will find that if you don't fill in the silence with words, your prospects and customers will. This gives you a better opportunity to find out where you stand and what else needs to occur to consummate a sale.

Lesson 77
Would You Like Some Fries with that Shake?

Two of the quickest ways to increase your sales productivity is to employ the techniques of cross-selling and up-selling. The McDonald's chain of fast food restaurants does it best by teaching their affiliates to always ask, "Would you like an order of fries with that shake?"…or, "Could I interest you in a hot apple pie to go along with your meal?"

Most vendors today offer a suite of complimentary products. As such, getting in the door with one solution can pave the way to have other conversations about additional opportunities. Broadening your sales conversations to include these other opportunities is traditionally known as cross-selling, selling across product lines. Up-selling is similar in terms of broadening the opportunity. Essentially, up-selling is a strategy for leveraging smaller successes to penetrate into higher and more strategic levels within your accounts.

Cross-selling and up-selling both are mindsets that come from focusing on the implications of a problem, not just the problem itself. This brings us back to the PAS positioning model that was introduced earlier. If a customer walks into a McDonald's fast food restaurant, they do so because they have a need. They want something to eat. Of course, when they order something to eat, it makes sense that they might also want something to drink. And let's not forget dessert. This seems relatively straightforward for those people who work for McDonald's, doesn't it? But if you sell office furniture, then you probably have customers who are interested in buying desks and chairs. But if someone is interested in desks and chairs, they might also need bookcases, file cabinets, or other accessories that would further compliment their office.

The same mindset exists when you are trying to penetrate more deeply into your customer accounts. If you sell technology services, for example, and you solve a difficult network problem for one of your customers, your success can create other opportunities to provide additional services in the future.

I encourage sellers to make this notion of cross-selling and up-selling a conscious practice. With minimal effort on your part, you can create all kinds of additional opportunities by broadening the scope of your sale into other areas where your product or service might also add value. One approach is to be direct and simply ask the prospect if they would like some "fries" with their "shake." One can otherwise take a much softer tack by asking, "Mr. Prospect, since we are currently working with you to solve this very important problem, would it also make sense to have some conversation about the two additional projects that are being planned for next quarter?"

Lesson 78
Wanting a Better Price Isn't Always an Objection

We must always remember that buyers will object to the price of your proposal whether they have a price objection or not. That's what buyers are supposed to do. Particularly in today's market, buyers have been conditioned to try and negotiate the price down even if they don't think it's too high.

Why does this happen? It happens because people in the buyer's organization will never forgive him if he doesn't *try* to negotiate a lower price, but they will always forgive him if he doesn't actually get it.

Whether you treat the prospect's request for a lower price as an objection or something else has a lot to do with your perspective about your product and its position in the marketplace.

> If you think your product or service is over-priced, then your buyer's request for a lower price will sound like an objection.

If you think your product or service is over-priced, then your buyer's request for a lower price will sound like an objection. If, on the other hand, you believe the value being offered by your product or service more than justifies its price (which is where you should be in your negotiations), then you are in a strong position to either stand firm or negotiate a reasonable discount.

Lesson 79
Delivering Bad News Gracefully

In large deals, after you have already negotiated your absolute lowest best and final price, what do you do when the prospect starts hitting you up for additional discounts? Do you say, "No," or do you just give them everything they ask for?

Giving prospects everything they ask for is a bad strategy because the more you give, the more they'll want—until the deal becomes bad business for you and your company. But for salespeople, saying, "No," can be a frightening proposition because it represents that moment of truth in the sale where prospects will either move forward with a decision to purchase, or turn their backs and walk away.

It's critical that sellers learn to say "No," because prospects have been conditioned to push harder and harder for additional discounts until there is no more. Therefore, salespeople must know when to give a little extra to consummate a sale, and they also have to know when to say, "There is no more to give." But this doesn't make delivering the actual bad news any easier.

Saying "No" is difficult because it puts you on the other side of the argument. The prospect is essentially asking for your help, in the form of either a lower price or free add-ons, and you are essentially telling them, "No, I am no longer in a position to help you."

Communicating that you are "no longer willing to help" is not the message you want to convey at the end of a sale, especially when you are trying to make prospects feel comfortable enough to pull the trigger on a favorable decision. Fortunately there is an alternative, a way that allows you to deliver bad news gracefully.

The technique is simple. If a prospect asks for something that is unreasonable or beyond what you are willing to include as part of the sales transaction, you simply start your response with, "I'd be happy to…" For example, suppose you've already negotiated down to your best and final price, and the prospect says, "We need another 10% off the price." Using this technique, you would confidently respond by saying, "I'd be happy to give you another 10% off the price." Now, this is not the entire answer because we are assuming that the buyer is wanting something you are not willing to provide.

Here's the rest of the answer. After saying, "I would be happy to take another 10% off the price," you simply add, "but here's the problem. We don't have another 10% discount to give." You should reiterate that you would like to earn their business very much, but you should also be very direct in explaining that there is no extra 'fluff' built into the price from which to provide additional discounts.

> It's critical that sellers learn to say "No," because prospects have been conditioned to push harder and harder for additional discounts until there is no more.

When you deliver the bad news gracefully, you no longer have to be the bad guy. That's the beauty of this technique. You no longer have to be the one who says, "No, I am no longer willing to help you." While this approach allows you to be very direct in communicating that there is no extra room for discounting, you are softening the blow. You can still provide value to your customers by suggesting, "Mr. Prospect, if budget is the issue, perhaps we could remove certain line items from the proposal to reduce the bottom line price." Or, "Since your project includes a second and third phase, perhaps we could bundle the entire purchase together to make the deal size bigger, which would create some room to provide additional discounts."

This technique for delivering bad news gracefully has practical applications in real life too. For example:

"Son, I would be happy to do your math homework…but here's the problem. I'm not the one who will be taking the math test on Friday."

"Honey, I'd be happy to buy you a new diamond necklace…but here's the problem. Spending that much money on jewelry would mean we'd have to dip into the kid's college education fund."

"Jim, I would love to play golf on Saturday…but here's the problem. I already offered to take my kids to Six Flags on Saturday."

You will find that there is a huge difference between saying, "No," and saying, "I would be happy to, but…" Simply rephrasing your response allows you to deliver your bad news more gracefully. At the end of the day, you will be much more successful in sales (and in life) if you position your words so that you spend less time on the other side of the argument.

Lesson 80
Sometimes Nothing Works

In my business, I am always on the lookout for creative sales and marketing ideas. During the recent Christmas holiday season, I happened on an idea that I thought was particularly creative.

Perhaps you have heard of the charitable toy drive at Christmas called "Toys for Tots." Well, being charity-minded myself at Christmas, and always interested in new ideas, I was intrigued when I read about a local promotion at a topless club here in Atlanta. They were running a toy drive and were calling it "Toys for Ta-Tas."

Apparently, this club was getting in on the holiday spirit by offering patrons free admission with the donation of a toy. "This is a limited time special offer," I explained to my wife. "And it's for a good cause," I pleaded. Laura apparently didn't share the same sense of charity because she intimated that my "toys" would be better off staying at home. Even though I consider myself a pretty good salesperson, there comes a time when we all have to face the reality that sometimes nothing works.

Lesson 81
Dealing with Rejection

The fear of rejection is by far the most difficult part of selling. Even the strongest-willed salespeople feel vulnerable to the impending risk that prospects or customers might say, "No, thank you."

Without the risk of rejection, selling would be easy. Virtually anyone could pick up the telephone to prospect new accounts. It would also be easy to pose the hard questions to qualify opportunities and to ask for the order at the end of a sale. But since risk will always be part of the selling landscape, the question salespeople must wrestle with is how best to deal with rejection.

There are lots of ways people try to deal with rejection. One way is to just curb your emotional downswings by pretending that everything is always great! There is an old adage that says: "If you are being run out of town, get in front of the crowd and act like it's a parade." Just thinking about this creates a mental picture that makes me smile. But in all honesty, I was never very good at pretending that everything was "great" when it wasn't.

> Even the strongest-willed salespeople feel vulnerable to the impending risk that prospects or customers might say, "No, thank you.

Through my own career experiences, I have decided that the best way to deal with rejection in sales is to be rejected less frequently. The more often you win, the less rejection you have to face. Winning more frequently also increases your self-esteem, which will help buoy your confidence when you do lose an important sale. Isn't it true that the best time to make a sales call is after you've just closed a big sale? The opposite is also true. Sellers tend to feel most vulnerable right after they've been rejected.

My objective here is not to insult your intelligence. Of course, it's easier to deal with rejection when you win a sale. But it's also easier to deal with the possibility of rejection when you reduce your risk of failure throughout the sales process. That's why I invested so much time dealing with the issue of risk reduction in my first book. In my view, the most effective way to limit your risk of failure is to increase your probability of success in the account. Conversely, the easiest way to increase your probability of success is to reduce your risk. Because of this belief, I am one of the few sales trainers that addresses this issue of risk. Historically, sales trainers and sales managers have relied on the fact that selling is a numbers game. They figure risk just comes with the territory. I believe that selling is not just "a numbers game," and those salespeople who reduce their risk by improving their strategic sales skills can achieve higher levels of success. By the way, in keeping with the theme of this book, if you do give yourself a one-percent advantage over your competitors, you also reduce your risk of rejection.

Lesson 82
Ignorance is not Bliss

Not knowing exactly where you stand in the sale is a weak position for any salesperson. If problems are brewing in one of your accounts, you need to know about them in order to have an opportunity to respond. Likewise, if good news is on the horizon, and you are about to win the sale, you will want to know about this as well.

Traditional sales thinking suggests that the best way to find out where you stand in the sale is simply to ask your customers. The problem is, just because we want to find out the status of our sales, doesn't mean customers will automatically share complete and accurate information. Ironically, traditional sales methods teach sellers to pose questions about the status of their accounts in a way that actually causes prospects and customers to share less. But causing prospects to share less information is diametrically opposed to our objective of finding out exactly where we stand in relation to making a sale.

Salespeople have been conditioned to ask questions positively. In my first book, *Secrets of Question Based Selling*, we characterized this as asking questions with a positive disposition. As an example, it's common for sellers to ask positive closing questions like: "Mr. Prospect, are we still in good shape to wrap this deal up by the end of the month?"

> Just because we want to find out the status of our sales, doesn't mean customers will share complete and accurate information.

Say this out loud. It sounds positive, doesn't it? You can almost feel your head bobbing up and down as if to encourage the prospect to give a more positive response. But there's an inherent problem with this approach. Positive questions are not more likely to generate positive responses. In fact, just the opposite happens. Positively dispositioned questions cause prospects and customers to share less information, and less accurate information.

Another mistake is to assume better relationships will cause customers to share more openly. Most of the prospects and customers you deal with on a daily basis are honest people. Most of the salespeople I teach are honest, too. But maybe you aren't as honest as you think. For example, if your boss invited you to his house for dinner, and his wife, after preparing a seven-course meal, asked, "What did you think of my cooking?" Assume for a moment that it was the worst food you have ever put in your mouth. Would you be honest and tell her so? Of course you wouldn't—because people don't like to share bad news. It would be much easier to either say something neutral or tell a little fib that conveniently dodged the issue.

Prospects and customers don't like to be the bearers of bad news any more than you do. Therefore, what do you think happens when an enthusiastic salesperson poses a positively dispositioned question to a potential customer, like, "So, do you think we're still in good shape to wrap this deal up by the end of the month?"

What do you think the salesperson in this scenario wants to hear? Judging from the way they asked their question, he or she obviously wants to hear good news. You can feel it in the way the question gets delivered. But, what if bad news of some kind is brewing in the account? What if the budget has been slashed or the incumbent vendor has come back with a revised proposal that management really likes? While some customers are willing to share this information, others will play it close to the vest by saying something neutral like, "We are still working through some issues, but we'll keep you posted."

There are two reasons customers don't like to share bad news. One is that it just doesn't feel good to tell a salesperson they are not going to win the sale. Customers are well aware that a salesperson's livelihood is based on commissions, and telling someone that their income will be negatively impacted ranks right up there with telling the boss's wife that her cooking was dreadful. The other reason customers don't like to share bad news with sellers is that a fair number of salespeople go berserk upon hearing bad news. "What do you mean the budget got slashed? You told me this deal was going to be approved! We need to meet with your manager right now!" You may not do this to customers, but there are plenty other salespeople who just won't accept "No" for an answer.

Salespeople go berserk upon hearing bad news.

Consequently, it's safer and more comfortable for potential buyers to hold salespeople at arms-length, rather than share bad news.

Even when good news is brewing in your account, positively dispositioned questions are still less productive. That's because your positive phraseology discourages prospects and customers from sharing accurate information. To illustrate, suppose a purchase order had already been cut when an eager salesperson calls to follow up on the sale, asking, "Mr. Prospect, do you think we're still in good shape to wrap this deal up by the end of the month?" Many customers, knowing they have an eager salesperson on the hook, will play coy and say, "Well, I suppose I *might* be able to push it through...if you include some additional discounts and free consulting services."

As a salesperson, I want prospects to share their thoughts, feelings, and concerns. If bad news is brewing in one of my accounts, I want to know about it. If there's good news, and the customer is ready to move forward with a purchase, I want to know about that, too. That's why I teach salespeople to probe for both good news and bad news. The specific technique is called neutralizing the disposition of your questions.

Neutralize Your Questions to Increase Productivity

My goal when asking about the status of a prospective account is simple: I want to know where the sale currently stands and what needs to happen to move the opportunity forward. That's why I ask very few positively dispositioned questions. Instead, I ask questions that make it easy for prospects to share both good news and bad. Given the last scenario, where the salesperson wanted to know the status of a sale, here's the closing question I would ask:

> **Salesperson**: "Mr. Prospect, are we still in good shape to wrap this deal up by the end of the month, or do you think something might cause it to get pushed out?"

Prospects don't like to share bad news. But, if the budget was indeed cut or the sale was in jeopardy for some other reason, if you are willing to ask for bad news, most prospects will tell you. They will say something like, "Well, I think we might have a budget problem."

"A budget problem?" I would ask. "How do you mean?" Again, most customers will share bad news if you are open to hearing it. I should make the point that I don't actually want to hear bad news. I would much rather hear that every deal is on the verge of closing. But when there is a problem brewing in one of my accounts, I *do* want to know about it. You should want to know too.

When good news is pending in one of your accounts, something else happens. Remember the earlier example where the purchase order had already been cut. Not knowing the status, I would once again ask, "Are we still in good shape to wrap this deal up by the end of the month, or do you think something might cause it to get pushed out?"

While most people don't like to be the bearers of bad news, they love to deliver good news. "No…no, I've got the PO right here. My boss came in first thing this morning and signed it. We're done!"

Critics of this technique (neutralizing the disposition of your questions to probe for both good news and bad) might argue that introducing the negative gives the prospect an *out*. While that might be true, I would counter that most prospects already know they don't have to buy from you. In fact, I would assert that very few purchases happen because the key players in an important account decide, "We pretty much have to buy from XYZ Company because their salesperson didn't give us an out."

Your questioning strategy is fundamental to your success in sales. If you ask "hopeful" questions, you encourage prospects and customers to respond with less, and less accurate, information. If you make it a point to ask for both good news and bad, however, you are much more likely to find out exactly where you stand in the sale.

Lesson 83
You Can Learn More from Failure than Success

Why do salespeople who are struggling always lament about price, resource shortages, lack of marketing, and management deficiencies? Perhaps if these salespeople took an inward look at their own sales strategies, they would discover that issues like price, resources, marketing, and management may not be the problem at all. In fact, could it be possible (for any of us) that some of the challenges we face on a daily basis are self-inflicted—in which case, the best way to address these challenges might be to improve ourselves?

There is no doubt that we as salespeople can learn from our successes. When something goes well, we want to repeat the strategy, the behavior, and the corresponding result. Building upon one's successes is an admirable goal. But, while we can learn from success, we can learn even more if we take some time out of our busy schedules to better understand our losses.

Reviewing your losses can be a painful exercise. But loss reviews can also be very productive. The problem is, it's difficult to justify spending time sitting around and thinking about lost opportunities. It's easier just to point to something beyond our control as the reason for losing, particularly in a multi-faceted sale. Sometimes we blame corporate headquarters. Other times, we point fingers at someone else on our sales team. We even blame our competitors for being less than honest, or blame the customer for being too dumb to recognize that our proposal most closely met their needs.

Does your sales team hold formal loss reviews? Most sales organizations don't. What's fun about reviewing why a sale was lost, especially if the loss could have been prevented by our own mistakes along the way?

The purpose of holding loss reviews is not to assign blame. That only causes dissension among the troops and perpetuates problems in future sales. Instead, the reason to reflect back on our failures is the valuable insight one gains from asking, "What could I have done better in the last opportunity?" ...and "What can I do differently next time?" No matter who was actually at fault, the real question is, what could have been done to recognize potential problems sooner or prevent them altogether?

> "What could I have done better in the last opportunity?" "What can I do differently next time?"

Barry Manilow, the well-known singer-songwriter, said it best in the opening lyrics for a song he wrote called, "The Other Ninety-Nine." He writes:

I learned more from failure,
than I learned from success.
I learned from "No, Thank You,"
so much more than from "Yes,"
I learned to be willing,
to lead with my chin.
And if I were willing to lose,
...I could win.

Loss reviews will never be fun. Celebrating success, now that's fun! But thinking strategically about missed opportunities is one of the most powerful exercises a salesperson or sales organization can undertake because you *will* learn more from failure than you will from success. Understanding your weaknesses so that you can better position yourself to win the sale next time will make the time invested in loss reviews well worth the effort.

Lesson 84
There is no "Other Side" of the Sale

After my first book was released, one of my former customers read it, liked it, and suggested that I write a book about the other side of the sales transaction—strictly for buyers. In essence, they wanted me to create a strategy to help buyers deal more effectively with salespeople.

On the surface, the idea sounded like a good one. But as I thought more about it, I realized that there is no "other side" of a sales transaction.

Traditional sales thinking tends to talk about buyers and

> Buyers and sellers have the same objective when it comes to the actual sale—working toward a mutual exchange of value.

sellers as if they are opposing forces. But if you think about what the buyer and the seller are actually trying to accomplish, you will find that there are more similarities than differences in their goals. In fact, in most sales, the buyer and the seller are working towards the same objective—a mutual exchange of value.

To illustrate, let's suppose you were interested in purchasing a car that I was advertising in the local newspaper. In this scenario, I am of course the seller, and you are the buyer. You would want what I have (the car), and I would want what you have (money). From an analytical perspective, we would both be working toward the same objective. We would be trying to agree on terms that would allow an exchange of equivalent value. If we agreed on a price of $20,000, for example, the seller would be agreeing to trade $20,000 worth of value (in the car), for $20,000 worth of value (in cash). The buyer would also be agreeing to trade $20,000 worth of value, for $20,000 worth of value. And both want to feel that they are getting a good deal.

Buyers and sellers have different perspectives to be sure, but they both have the same objective when it comes to the actual sale—working toward a mutual exchange of value. Therefore, if buyers and sellers are both trying to accomplish the same thing, we must conclude that there is no "other side" of the sale.

Lesson 85
Some Deals Aren't Worth Chasing

Several months ago, I was in Washington, DC to deliver a QBS sales training program, and one of the attendees came to the front of the room during the afternoon break to ask my advice on a sales situation. This salesperson, Peter, explained that one of his key prospect accounts, after evaluating his software, apparently lost their sense of urgency, to the point where they were no longer returning his calls. Peter added that his internal champion recently left the account, the prospect's budget had been slashed, and the incumbent vendor just invited the key executives in the account on a boondoggle trip to the World Series. "What can I do to turn this deal around?" Peter asked.

To me, the question Peter should have been asking himself was, "Does it make sense to continue chasing this deal?"

Some prospects are not going to buy from you. Whether

they don't recognize the existence of a need, they support another solution, or they have had a bad experience with your company in the past, some prospects just aren't going to buy from you, no matter what.

This is not what the typical salesperson's killer instinct wants to hear. We want to kick-ass and take names at accounts in our respective sales territories, and we want to turn every opportunity into a successful conquest. Nonetheless, sellers have to recognize that not every opportunity is worth pursuing, and chasing deals that don't have a reasonable probability of closure becomes a worthless waste of time, energy, and selling resources.

> Chasing deals that don't have a reasonable probability of closure becomes a worthless waste of time, energy, and selling resources.

Furthermore, we must realize that every sale has an opportunity cost. In the old days, whenever a sale closed, the manager would ring the bell and everyone in the office would cheer. Now, the objective has changed from just closing sales to maximizing the overall revenue in a territory. And, since most sellers cannot pursue every opportunity in their territory, chasing bad business usually means other more lucrative opportunities are left unattended.

Essentially, there are two ways to maximize your opportunity in sales. One is to focus your selling efforts on expanding the size and scope of potential deals. The other is to minimize any wasted effort. This means better qualifying accounts and cutting your losses if the expected return on your sales investment doesn't justify a continued effort—which might have been the case in Peter's scenario.

Lesson 86
Thank You... Mitsubishi

In the spring of 1996, I asked my wife Laura, "Would you be absolutely opposed to having one of those big screen televisions in the den?"

While she was noticeably unenthusiastic about the idea, she responded somewhat neutrally saying that no, she wasn't "absolutely opposed." That sounded like a green light to me. So the next day, I went out and bought a brand new 46-inch Mitsubishi big screen. As you might imagine, Laura has been much less neutral in her responses ever since.

After three months of big screen bliss, a power surge in our neighborhood caused an electrical spike, which shorted out the electronics inside the television. A loud snap and a blue flash came from behind the base unit, and our brand new Mitsubishi went dead.

Since it was still under warranty, I contacted the local service center and they promptly came out and picked it up. They estimated that it would take five to seven days to repair and return the TV, which seemed reasonable.

After seven days passed, I called the repair center to follow up. The service manager explained that two replacement parts had been ordered, but only one had been received. The other part apparently was on back order. "On back order until when?" I asked. The service manager didn't know but he promised to find out and call me back. Within minutes, he called and told me the second part was back ordered until November. "November?" I was shocked! It was only May, and the thought of waiting six months to have my TV back seemed less than reasonable.

I promptly lobbed a call into Mitsubishi's national parts department. The woman who answered pulled my order number up on her computer and confirmed that part #624537-B was indeed on back order until November. She explained that there was nothing she could do to expedite the process, since Mitsubishi parts were manufactured overseas. I thanked her for the information and then asked, "What would you do if you were in my predicament?"

"I would probably escalate this to Customer Relations," she said.

Within seconds, I was on the phone with Mitsubishi's Consumer Relations department in New York City. "Hello, this is Marsha," the woman announced. "How can I help you?"

I briefly explained my predicament, and she too called up my account on her computer and once again confirmed that the part we needed was on back order for six months.

"Marsha," I asked, "By any chance, do you have young children?"

"Yes," she replied, "I have two boys...five and three (years old)."

"I have two daughters," I said. (We were bonding.) Then, I explained, "Marsha, here's the real problem. Every night, before I tuck my girls into bed, I have to explain that the reason they can't watch a video is because daddy bought a Mitsubishi."

"Oh no," Marsha moaned empathetically. My comment had obviously hit close to home.

"As I see it, there are three options. Mitsubishi can either replace my television with a brand new one, remove the part in question from a brand new television and put it in my TV, or you can cut me a refund check so I can go out and purchase a Sony."

"Mr. Freese, let me see what I can do," Marsha said.

That conversation occurred on Monday. By Friday of that same week, our 46-inch big screen television was fully operational and back in our den. It just goes to show that when resolving a standoff, it can be much more effective to forge common ground with the person you're dealing with, rather than getting upset and increasing the harshness of your demands.

Lesson 87
To Enhance Performance... Improve Thyself

The whole idea of self-improvement and self-development is relatively new. In the fifties and sixties, people didn't invest a lot of time thinking about long-term goals or strategic objectives. Life was much simpler then. Dad went to work in his long-term job, mom stayed home with the kids, family time was a regular activity, and everyone looked forward to a better tomorrow.

Today, we often find ourselves being ruled by the hustle and bustle of our daily environment. Mom and dad both work, the kids have to be shuttled back and forth between their school and social activities, and the overall pace of life has increased significantly. A similar trend has accelerated the pace of the professional selling environment. Sales organizations are expecting more of their people, asking them to work harder and to work smarter. As a result, the workplace is a more stressful environment, and in many cases, we wonder whether or not success is even within our grasp.

To me, the biggest breakthrough in self-development is the realization that individuals have the power to control their own destiny. Success is rarely an accident. Instead, it's the people who work the hardest and make sound decisions that end up being successful. To that end, people have started to take control of their own lives. Rather than blame external factors, people today are taking control by looking inward for opportunities to improve themselves, their businesses, and their quality of life.

> Salespeople who feel good about themselves tend to outsell those who don't.

For sellers, one of the by-products of self-improvement is the resulting motivation that enhances sales performance. Good technique is important, but it has also become clear that salespeople who feel good about themselves tend to outsell those who don't. Therefore, let's take an inward look at some of the things salespeople can do to increase their selling effectiveness.

There are essentially two things you can do to try and motivate yourself. One is to simply wish things were different. But passive hopefulness is not something that leads to a positive change, so let's not spend a lot of time there. The other way to motivate yourself is to do something about changing the status quo. That's where a few ideas from a distant thinker might just be the catalyst you need to step outside the box of what feels most comfortable, and into a world where you find yourself being more effective.

Start by Getting Organized

A place for everything, and everything in its place! That should be the motto of every salesperson. But it's not. A surprising number of salespeople would argue that they don't have time to get organized. I say, make the time. Being organized changes the way you feel about yourself. It also empowers you to feel more prepared and more productive. Think about the last time you cleaned out your office. Didn't you feel accomplished afterward? By removing the various piles from the top of your desk, updating your files, and throwing away hundreds of pounds of outdated paperwork, who wouldn't feel more accomplished? Getting organized gives people a feeling of accomplishment and people who feel more accomplished tend to be more productive.

Here are my six rules for staying organized:

1.) If something is not currently being worked on, then it should not be on your desk—period! That's why they make in-baskets. Having lots of pending projects on your desk only takes your focus off the things that are most important. Having a full desk can also demoralize you when the volume of work makes it look like you can never catch up.

2.) Take anything that is not going to be dealt with in the short term out of your in-basket. Create a system for prioritizing longer-term projects, and then keep those projects in a place where they can be easily accessed without contributing to the clutter.

3.) Always clear your desk before leaving the office. This practice ensures that you will get a fresh start next time you are there.

4.) Resist using your office as a storage facility. If you are like most people, you have business records or personal files you want to save from previous years. That's fine. But it's a good idea to store them away from your immediate workspace. It's a mistake to fill your desk with so much paraphernalia from the past that you don't have enough room for current tasks.

> Getting organized gives you a feeling of accomplishment and people who feel more accomplished tend to be more productive.

5.) Establish throw away criteria. Wardrobe consultants say that if you haven't worn a garment in the last two years, you should get rid of it. The same should be true in your office. Therefore, allocate some time on a weekly basis to clean up and clean out.

6.) Start noticing other people's offices. Humans are judgmental. We can't help it. So, let me ask, what impression do you form when you see someone else's office in disarray? When I see a messy desk, I think, "unorganized person." Fortunately, the opposite is true. A clean and well-organized office leads people to assume higher levels of professionalism. The question is, what impression do you want your office to convey?

Become Knowledgeable in Areas where You Feel
Most Vulnerable

Everyone has certain areas of expertise where we feel confident and self-assured, and we look for opportunities to share this expertise with others. Likewise, we all have weaknesses where we have little aptitude or experience, and it's only natural to try and avoid these areas.

When I started selling computer hardware, for example, I didn't understand network topologies. Customers would start talking about their Ethernet or Token-Ring protocols, and I was lost. Once I realized that my own lack of knowledge was making me feel uncomfortable, I figured I had two choices. I could either wish things were different or do something to change the status quo. With a concentrated effort that consisted of reading books about the different network protocols and spending a day in the lab with a Systems Engineer, my knowledge base increased dramatically. So did my confidence. Soon I could trade networking buzzwords with the best of them.

One of the surest ways to impact your own performance is to increase your knowledge base. This in turn will increase your confidence when dealing with prospects and customers. Here's a simple exercise that will help you implement this concept. First, make a list of your strengths. What are your current areas of expertise? Include everything, even if it's just your knowledge of how to unjam the copy machine. Next, make a list of those areas that make you feel most vulnerable. Which subjects make you the most nervous when they come up in your sales conversations? What questions are you least prepared to handle? The goal is to identify your weaknesses and then systematically transfer them over to your list of strengths. If you commit yourself, the long-term pay back of tackling just one weakness per month is enormous.

Always Expend the Most Effort

Make it a point to outwork your competition, including other members of your sales team. If other salespeople are calling six new prospects per day, you should make every effort to contact eight. If other salespeople remain at the office until 6:30pm, then you should stay until 7:00pm. Someone has to succeed in sales; it might as well be the person who puts in the greatest effort. (We talked about this earlier in Lesson 9.)

Improve Your Physical Fitness

Are you a self-conscious person? Let me ask it differently. Do you check yourself in the mirror at least once a day (like the rest of us)? Then you are a self-conscious person. It's another one of those natural human qualities. Like it or not, we care about what other people think. When we look better, we also tend to feel better. And when a salesperson feels better, they tend to sell more.

One of the most effective ways to improve your sales performance is to improve your physical fitness—and you can start by losing a few pounds. Doesn't have to be a lot. If you can shed five, ten, or fifteen pounds, you will experience a burst of confidence that will make you virtually unstoppable in your efforts to tackle the next challenge. People are motivated by personal successes, and for most people, losing weight is a huge confidence-inducing event.

Sticking to a regular exercise routine is another confidence builder. Do you exercise regularly? Many people don't. Just remember, it's always going to be more difficult to make quota when you are not feeling well, or when you're dead.

Volunteer for a Worthy Cause

When you're not putting extra hours in at the office, try volunteering for a good cause—Habitat for Humanity, for example. Making someone else feel special is a terrific way to boost your own confidence. In fact, most volunteers would confess that they get more out of volunteering their efforts than the person they are actually helping.

> It's always going to be more difficult to make quota when you are not feeling well, or when you're dead.

So, here's an idea. Next time you want to engage your sales organization in a team building exercise, try volunteering the entire group for an activity that helps someone in need. Not only will your team experience the togetherness that comes from a team building exercise, they will also feel the joy that comes from making the world a better place.

Summary Point

Every time you improve yourself personally, you also improve yourself professionally. This is one of the great secrets to success in business. Show me someone who has taken steps to raise their confidence and fulfill their inner self, and I will show you someone who will perform at higher levels in their respective business environment.

Lesson 88
Have a Passion for What You Do

Passion is another one of the secret ingredients that separates top performing salespeople from the rest of the masses. We can talk about strategy, hard work, and doing the right things until we are blue in the face, but at the end of the day, people who truly believe in what they are doing are the ones who will most likely succeed in sales.

Some people live by the saying, "Life is short." Others abide by the adage, "Lead, follow, or get out of the way." I'm sure that you've heard similar clichés. Maybe you have your own motto. Mine is, "Do what you love, and love what you do." Motivation comes from within, and the passion you have to excel will ultimately determine whether you succeed or fail.

Call it what you want...determination, resolve, fortitude, conviction, or tenacity. Inside every great leader burns a passion for what they believe in. Martin Luther King, Jr., for example, the great civil rights leader from the sixties didn't say, "I have a strategic plan." Rather, he said, "I have a dream!" He cared deeply about his dream and was totally committed to it.

Some people are born passionate. The rest of us have to develop our passions. So, what are you passionate about? Do you believe in yourself? Do you believe in the products and services you offer, and in your company? The answer to these questions is already known—by your prospects and customers, your boss, your co-workers, even your family and friends. If you find you are just going through the motions, however, then you have an opportunity to make changes that will impact your entire outlook as well as your sales performance. Best of all, if you become one of those salespeople who truly believes in what they do, you will discover that selling doesn't feel like work at all.

Lesson 89
Practice by Being a Better Buyer

There's an old saying that you don't actually get what you deserve, you get what you negotiate. This is certainly true in professional sales. You already know that customers who are tough during price negotiations tend to get extra discounts and special favors, while other customers who are less aggressive end up paying full price. Sometimes all it takes is a willingness to ask for the better deal.

One of the best ways to become a better salesperson is to practice being a better buyer. Knowing how buyers think can give you a unique advantage when you are working toward a mutual exchange of value.

When I am the buyer, I always ask for discounts. Not every request I make is granted, but you would be amazed at how much extra value is available just for the asking. In fact, my favorite question to ask is, "Do you offer a preferred customer discount?" Whether you are shopping for a new laptop or garden supplies, virtually every business offers special discounts to preferred customers. Therefore, the answer to the question, "Do you offer a preferred customer discount?" is almost always going to be, "Yes." My next question then is, "What do I need to do to become a preferred customer?" At that point, it's difficult for a salesperson or manager to look you in the eye and tell you that you are not "preferred." It's easier for them just to give you the extra discount.

Another strategy for negotiating additional discounts is to point to the cost of an item and ask, "Is this your best price?" If there is any room for a discount, the salesperson either has to lie or admit that yes, there is a better price. Everyone uses this strategy when shopping for cars, but you'd be surprised how many businesses can offer a better price if you are willing to ask. This question works particularly well when checking into a hotel. If you ask the clerk, "Is this your best rate?", you might be surprised how much leeway they have to offer you a better deal.

Just by showing a little confidence as a buyer, many of the clerks you encounter will respond by pushing the little orange button on the register that triggers an additional discount. One time, a clerk even asked me, "Which one of our discounts would you like?" Without missing a beat, I said, "The biggest discount you can offer." She immediately reached out and pushed one of the buttons on her register, only this time it was the little pink button. Frankly, I would have been satisfied with the orange button, but hey, she asked.

Lesson 90
Make Your Business Seem Bigger

Corporate giants like AT&T, General Electric, Westinghouse, and IBM have a huge advantage—they have name recognition. If you sell well-branded products from an internationally recognized source, you should leverage your product or company's reputation to the hilt. But what if you don't sell for a widely recognized brand name or company? What if you recently accepted a sales position with a start-up company or you are out there trying to make it on your own? Then, the lack of market awareness is likely to be one of your biggest initial hurdles.

According to the Small Business Administration (SBA), ninety-five percent of all newly established companies close their doors and go out of business within the first two years of operations. Consequently, customers who make decisions that depend on the success of these start-up ventures are often left holding the bag.

If it's true that some prospects perceive that dealing with bigger companies translates into safer decisions, then smaller companies may be wise to look at different ways to make their businesses seem bigger and more established.

Fortunately, there are a number of strategies you can employ to make your small business seem less small, and therefore, less risky. For example, you can:

- Secure an "800" number. For a relatively small investment (usually only a couple dollars per month), you can enhance the prospect's perception of your business but putting yourself in the same class with other corporations who boast "800" number status.

- Make your business address sound more like a business. Hewlett Packard, the Coca Cola Company, Mindspring, and Mrs. Fields are just a few of the legendary corporate success stories that started in the founder's house or garage. But that doesn't remove the need to sound credible in your own virtual business environment. That's why it might be smart to look at tailoring your business address either by using an official PO Box, or simply by adding a suite number to your home address. Be careful though. If you reside at 121 Willow Bay Court, you won't fool anyone by adding "Suite 300."

- Use an automated voice-mail system. While answering machines may be fine for home use, hearing a tape-recorded message tends to cheapen the caller's impression of your business. Now that most of the local telephone service providers offer automated voice-mail service on a subscription basis, it is wise to make the investment.

- In addition to securing an automated voice-mail service, you might also want to explore the use of sub-mailboxes. Most providers offer touch-tone features that give callers the ability to select between multiple different sub-mailboxes. This allows you to program an outgoing message to say, "If you would like to place an order, press 1. If you would like to leave a private voice-mail for Dean Sayers, press 2. If you would like to leave a message in ABC Company's general mailbox, press 3." You may also want to have someone else's voice on your company's initial greeting. Very few large businesses have the president's voice on the opening message.

- Be sure to let prospects know you're busy. Someone who is always available to answer their own phone is not perceived to be as valuable as someone else who is harder to reach. Techniques for letting people know you are busy include putting callers on hold for a few seconds while you finish whatever you were doing, even if it was just checking the fax machine. You will also seem busier if you schedule events (meetings, conference calls, etc.) at odd times. For example, you might say, "Mr. Jones, would you be available to get together later today at 2:15pm?"

My favorite idea for making a business "sound bigger" comes from an excerpt I saw in the *New York Post*. Apparently, a cunning young entrepreneur named Robert Laisert, a Media Consultant, was trying to break into the advertising industry on Madison Avenue. Since Robert didn't want customers to know he was operating the business out of his home, whenever calls came in after 8:00pm, he answered the phone by saying, "Security."

Lesson 91
Use Small Notepads to Capture Big Ideas

Salespeople are always thinking. If they aren't strategizing in their mind about account situations, they're thinking about their families or about pending projects at home. In fact, if you're like most salespeople, then all kinds of thoughts and ideas are constantly jumping around in your head.

Have you ever had an idea pop into your head that you knew was terrific, but then couldn't think of it later in the day? You rack your brain but whatever it was that popped into your head is unfortunately gone. Frankly, it happens to most of us, especially to those salespeople who are generating lots of new ideas. Wouldn't it be nice to somehow capture these fleeting thoughts as they occur rather than trusting your memory to have perfect recall?

There's a simple remedy for this, one that I learned from my dad. After he retired a few years ago, he started carrying a small notepad in his shirt pocket.

That way, whenever one of those fleeting thoughts would pop into his head, he pulled out his trusty pad and captured it instantly. At a cocktail party, when someone mentions that a new exhibit is coming to the local art gallery, if Dad is inter-

> Have you ever had an idea pop into your head that you knew was terrific, but then couldn't think of it later in the day?

ested, he takes out his notepad and writes it down. Or, he'll be out walking his dog and remember that Roger (his dog) needs a new flea collar, so he'll stop and write that down. Essentially, his notepad serves as a repository of ideas, reminders, and information, that with periodic review, helps him to maximize each and every day.

I didn't give the idea much credence at first—that is, until I put a small notepad on the nightstand next to my bed. When ideas popped into my head just before bedtime, or when I hopped out of the shower, I would write them down. Knowing that my ideas would be there in the morning gave me such incredible peace of mind that I put another small notepad in my car, and one in my briefcase. Don't tell any-one…but I also carry one in my shirt pocket—just like dear old dad. In just a few minutes every day, I can review my notes to capture and consolidate important information that might have otherwise been lost.

If your competitors don't keep a notepad on their night-stand or in their shirt pockets, then perhaps this is an idea that will give you a significant competitive advantage—hey, better write that one down.

Lesson 92
Calling in the Cavalry

There are certain times in your sales when it's appropriate to bring in your sales manager or a corporate executive to escalate the opportunity to a higher level. Escalating the sale is particularly useful when the sales process has stalled or you have reached some sort of impasse that a higher level manager might be able to help resolve. Be careful, though, because calling in the cavalry can also harm your selling efforts.

What if your manager is so impressive that customers and prospects want to deal directly with him or her in the future instead of you? In this scenario, introducing a higher-level person from your company into the mix could actually undermine your credibility in the sale. You can't blame the buyer. It's only natural for them to gravitate toward the more knowledgeable and competent resource.

A sales manager or executive can create similar problems during price negotiations. If you have already delivered your best and final price, you don't want your sales manager to show up and undermine your credibility by throwing out a lower price. But these situations happen all the time, especially when quarter-end is approaching and the pressure is on to bring in sales.

Don't get me wrong. I am not opposed to involving upper management in your selling opportunities. The truth is, there's almost nothing more powerful than the one-two punch of a salesperson who's in sync with their manager. But synchronization is essential. Rather than undermine your credibility, sales executives can build up the buyer's faith in you by reiterating key points you have already made. When prospective buyers hear the same recommendations from your manager that they have already heard from you, they tend to feel more comfortable. And when prospects feel more comfortable, they are more likely to pull the trigger on making a favorable purchase decision.

Introducing senior executives into your sales opportunities, such as the president, CEO, or the founder of your company, also carries with it a certain marquee value. One of my clients, Sun Microsystems, for example, gains tremendous sales leverage by having customers meet Sun's CEO, Scott McNealy. He is one of the most charismatic technology leaders in the Silicon Valley, so just listening to him articulate his vision for technology in the future makes it difficult for them to even think about buying another platform. Even if your company's CEO does not have the same name recognition as a Scott McNealy, customers still appreciate the fact that the person at the top of your organization cares enough about their business to be personally involved.

Lastly, introducing higher level managers into your sales opportunities can be a very effective strategy for finding out where you stand in the deal. But rather than allow your manager to come in with guns blazing, you should always make it a point to coach them on what to say (and what not to say) in the meeting. For example, I always wanted executives I introduced into the sales process to open the meeting by asking the customer: "What can I do to help you and your company be more successful?" Then, everyone on the sales team needs to shut up. If you are dealing with a qualified prospect, this simple question usually opens the floodgates of conversation because customers appreciate the escalated level of interest in their success.

Lesson 93
The Five-Week Rolling Forecast

Forecasting sales is part of the job. As long as there are sales objectives that must be met by month-end, quarter-end, or year-end, there will be a need to track deals and project results. Many of the sales forecasts being handed in to management are incomplete or just plain inaccurate, however. Opportunities that are forecasted with a ninety-five percent probability of closing end up slipping away, while other deals that were barely visible on the sales manager's radar screen mysteriously close. As a result, companies are going crazy trying to figure out how much product to manufacture, how to properly staff to meet contracted service obligations, and how to more effectively manage the sales organization.

The answer to date has always been to try and create a

better mousetrap—i.e. better forecasting tools. Companies pay incredible amounts of money to outside consultants, for example, to come in and teach sales organizations how to forecast more accurately. These consultants then bring in their sophisticated forecasting models (a fancy name for a spreadsheet), and parade the sales force through a series of three to five day training classes explaining how their tool is supposed to be used.

The theory behind these "sophisticated" spreadsheets is sound. If the entire sales organization uses the same criteria to determine the status of their accounts, *and* they are thorough in documenting each and every component of the sales process, *and* they complete these 'spreadsheets' in a timely manner, sales managers and corporate executives will benefit by gaining tremendous insight into their company's sales projections.

According to Michael Bader, however, Regional Vice President for Questra Corporation, a company that works with clients to implement sales automation software, eighty percent of all sales automation projects fail within the first twelve months. The reason is simple. Salespeople don't want to spend their time filling out fancy spreadsheets.

So, while the underlying theory may be sound, the practicality of using these forecasting tools is questionable. The traditional business establishment continues to puzzle over how to get salespeople to buy in. From the salesperson's perspective, filling out spreadsheets may benefit someone back at corporate headquarters, but if it doesn't help *me* to be more effective, then *I am* not going to invest the time. In fact, most sellers would argue that every minute they spend on paperwork takes away from their earning potential. How many companies calculate commissions based on whoever creates the best sales forecast? The answer is none. Then what's the incentive?

Please don't misinterpret my intent. I am not downplaying the need for accurate sales forecasts or suggesting they aren't important. They are! I am simply pointing out that providing salespeople with increasingly complex spreadsheets doesn't address the actual issue. A show of force won't address the issue either. Requiring sales forecasts to be handed in by a certain date may improve the timeliness of forecasts, but it does nothing to ensure accuracy. Let's be honest. Much of the information being entered into these spreadsheets is put in at the last minute just before forecasts are due. By this point, the individual salesperson's objective is simply to fill in the blanks and move on to something more productive. They figure most sales managers won't notice the details anyway.

And you know what? They're right. Most sales managers don't focus on the account detail. Instead, they aggregate the forecasted sales numbers of all their direct reports to see how close they are to hitting their own targets for the end of the month, quarter, or year. Hence the problem. If a salesperson isn't motivated to do the paperwork, and sales managers aren't going to use the account detail anyway, why bother investing the effort? All of this puts companies in a Catch-22 situation, where they depend on accurate sales forecasts to run their businesses, but traditional methods of forecasting are less than perfect.

I don't have a magic formula that eradicates this problem. But I do recommend to many of my clients that they split their sales forecast into two separate functions. First, because it's important to capture a view of each salesperson's pipeline for the next quarter or two, I support asking individual salespeople to create and update (on a monthly basis) their sales projections for the next six months. This provides sales managers with a longer-term view of anticipated sales activity so they can manage pipeline development and appropriately allocate resources. For this, you can use any forecasting model that documents account detail, deal size, and estimated timeframe for closure. Secondly, but perhaps even more critical for sales managers to meet their numbers and develop their sales teams, I would ask salespeople to create and update a five-week rolling forecast—to be used as a monitoring tool to track pending deals as they approach the end of the sales process.

> If a salesperson isn't motivated to do the paperwork, and sales managers aren't going to use the account detail anyway, why bother investing the effort?

The five-week rolling forecast is a summary document that serves as a radar screen for salespeople and their mangers to dynamically track forecasted opportunities as they move forward toward closure, or slip out into the future. If you ask salespeople to plug the deals they are tracking into a simple columnar format like the one on the next page, you end up with a picture of every deal that has a possibility of closing in the next five weeks.

FIVE-WEEK ROLLING FORECAST
Salesperson: J. Madison
XYZ Corporation

Prospect	Probability	9/9	9/16	9/23	9/30	10/6	Projected Revenue
ABB Industrial	50%	82K					41K
Caldwell Banker	90%	10K					9K
Colliers Cable	40%				20K		8K
D&G Printing	80%			15K			12K
Emory Hospital	90%			50K			45K
Georgia Pacific	80%				80K		64K
Southern Hotels	50%		16K				8K
Verizon Wireless	70%			30K			21K
Video Networks	80%					25K	20K
Total Anticipated Revenue							**228K**

Note: The projected revenue column is a statistical average that aggregates the expected revenue multiplied by its probability of closure.

For salespeople, this five-week forecasting tool requires minimal effort to update. Every week, the salesperson simply changes the dates at the top of each column and adjusts their deals forward or backward according to when they are expected to close. And, since you are asking for minimum effort from each salesperson, there is no longer an excuse for a lack of accuracy or incomplete information.

The five-week rolling forecast also addresses a significant problem for sales managers. Most companies forecast their sales through the end of a period, like the end of a month. When a deal slips beyond month-end, it usually drops off the forecast completely—in which case, you've heard the saying, "Out of sight, out of mind." When deals are no longer visible on the radar screen, the likelihood that they can be pulled back into the current month is significantly reduced. With the rolling forecast format, deals can still slip, but you gain the advantage of being able to see where they went.

The typical sales forecast tends to give a static picture. Someone takes the time to fill out the necessary paperwork, and all this information then lies dormant for 30 days until next month's paperwork is due. Since the rolling forecast is a dynamic tool, however, deals are either moving forward on the forecast (i.e. closer to closing), or they are being pushed out into the future. As a result, sales that always seem to be two weeks away from closing get flagged as they continue to be pushed out week after week. Sales managers also get the added benefit of increased accuracy, because it becomes apparent very quickly who on their sales teams knows the status of their account and who doesn't.

At the end of the day, a five-week rolling forecast gives salespeople and sales managers (both) a device that can help to plan an ongoing strategy for maximizing revenue.

Lesson 94
Crossing the Cultural Chasm

"It's a small world after all, …it's a small world after all, …it's a small world after all, …it's a small, small world." For me, the world became much smaller when I started delivering QBS Methodology Training Programs in London, Paris, Sydney, Lisbon, Frankfurt, and Ottawa, in addition to the events I deliver all over the United States.

As *my* world has grown smaller, I have learned many things about other cultures. For example, I have learned that it's considered uncouth to order French fries in France. I have learned that everyone doesn't drive their car on the "right" side of the street. I have also learned that when you encounter someone who does not speak English, talking louder and more emphatically does not help them to understand.

The need to embrace different cultures is underscored by the fact that we are now dealing in a global economy. Even if your company is not internationally diverse, you are no doubt dealing with other companies that are. Different cultures around the world are indeed different. This should not be too much of a surprise, since most of us are well aware that doing business in New York City is very different than doing business in Los Angeles or Alabama.

The key to being successful in diverse cultures is to be cordial to your environment. This means having a certain sensitivity to the customs and traditions of the people you are dealing with. In Asia, for example, when someone hands you a business card, it's considered polite to receive the card with two hands, holding the top corners between your forefingers and thumbs. I learned about this while training clients in the Pacific Rim. "What if you are already holding something in your hands?" I asked. The answer is, you put it down—as a sign of respect.

Since cultures are so different, I recommend that you not

pretend to be part of someone else's culture. Faking an accent or engaging in unfamiliar cultural gestures (like bowing) is generally frowned upon. Foreign nationals don't expect you to adopt their ways, they just want to feel that you are respectful of their heritage and traditions.

You can ensure success with unfamiliar cultures by doing some reconnaissance in advance. The travel section of your local bookstore, for example, has lots of books dealing with various cultural nuances all over the world. If you are doing business internationally, you should also try to team with somebody who understands the local language, customs, and culture. In addition to being able to more effectively communicate, partnering with someone local can save you lots of headaches (and money) in places where someone might otherwise try to take advantage of a foreigner.

Someone who understands the local culture can also help protect you from embarrassing situations. Case in point, last summer I traveled to Sydney, Australia to deliver QBS Methodology training for VERITAS Software's Asia/Pacific sales team. While I was in town, the biggest rugby match of the year was played between the Australian Wallabies and the New Zealand All-Blacks. For Australians, this was the Super Bowl equivalent for the sport of rugby. VERITAS purchased a block of seats, and everyone who participated in the sales conference was invited to attend the match.

Early on, the crowd at-large was supporting the Australians. That was understandable since the match was being played in Sydney, Australia. Some people in the VERITAS block, however, mostly those who were from New Zealand, were cheering for the All-Blacks. Craig Stevens, VERITAS's Vice

President for Asia/Pacific, wasn't sure who to cheer for, since he lived in San Francisco. So, he yelled out over his group asking, "Which team should I root for?" As Craig tells the story, the people around him immediately bust into laughter. Something was obviously amiss. Finally, a voice from several rows back called out, "We don't *root* for anybody here mate, we *barrack* for the green team." The Australians were in green. A few minutes later, the person next to Craig leaned over and explained that the word "root" in Australia means "to masturbate." Oops!

Lesson 95
Avoid Rush Hour Traffic at All Costs

At last, after many years of contemplation and consternation, I have identified the root of all evil—rush hour traffic. Battling the daily commute is the least productive and most stressful thing many sales professionals do, and they do it twice a day. Cellular telephones have helped, but it is still difficult to stay focused when the guy ahead of you is riding his brakes or the woman in the car beside you is taking rollers out of her hair.

Some people are lucky. They live in close proximity to their workplaces, and their daily commute takes only five or ten minutes at the most. Other people, who aren't so lucky, spend hundreds of hours each year in cars, on trains, and in buses, fighting their way to and from the office.

For salespeople especially, I'm a big proponent of taking

rush hour out of your life. It's congruent with what this entire book is about—differentiating yourself from the rest of the masses. But you can't differentiate yourself if you join the rat race with everyone else who leaves for work at seven o'clock in the morning and goes home at five. Commuting back and forth to work during the height of rush hour traffic means enduring extraordinarily long travel times to and from the office and expending all kinds of emotional energy in the process.

Rush hour traffic also removes your ability to control your own destiny. I'm sure we have all missed an important meeting or appointment because a fender-bender brought traffic to a dead stop on the highway.

> Battling the daily commute is the least productive and most stressful thing many sales professionals do, and they do it twice a day.

If you enjoy sitting in rush hour traffic or have some special circumstance that prevents you from avoiding it, then I cannot offer any further assistance and you should move on to the next lesson. If, however, if you have had enough, and would like to replace this part of your day with something more fulfilling and productive, then read on.

My advice for salespeople is simple—avoid rush hour traffic at all costs. Don't worry, rush hour will still happen without you. You just make a conscious decision not to participate. Salespeople often have the advantage of flexible schedules. With the exception of internal meetings, sellers aren't supposed to be in the office. Instead, they spend the bulk of their time on the telephone or out on appointments. So, if you need a telephone between the hours of 7:00am and 9:00am, either use your cell phone or set up an office in your home. The same strategy applies between the hours of 4:30pm and 6:30pm.

"But I have to be at the office at 8:30am to meet clients." That's fine. Leave your house at 6:00am (before rush hour begins). You will be on time for your appointment, and you'll have plenty of time to get organized, clean up, and strategize before your meeting—all productive time, I might add. The same is true when you are finished for the day. Whether you stay late or leave the office early, it doesn't matter, so long as you don't sentence yourself to the daily grind of having to fight through rush hour traffic.

Think about it this way. If you're stuck in traffic while your competitors have discovered that rush hour is non-productive time, then you are at a serious disadvantage. It's likely, however, that your competitors haven't figured this out yet—in which case, imagine what could happen if you put your travel time to good use while your competitors were stuck in rush hour traffic. You would certainly have a unique advantage.

Lesson 96
Learn to Laugh at Yourself

People today take themselves much too seriously. I'm sure you have heard or read that stress has become one of the leading causes of death in America. People are literally worrying their health away. Perhaps this shouldn't surprise us since we are managing serious careers, we have serious financial obligations, and given the fast-paced world in which we live, people are just more serious—especially salespeople. Rather than become another victim of the daily grind, you can deal with stress and increase your sales performance at the same time by lightening up and learning to laugh at yourself.

A career in sales can be an emotional roller-coaster ride. When things are going along well, we tend to get our hopes up. When things are not going well, however, we get discouraged. I struggled with the daily ups and downs of the sales process for quite a few years before realizing

> Becoming more serious usually made the situation worse and the onset of stress turned into a self-fulfilling prophecy.

that if we (as salespeople) are not in control of our own emotions, then it is very difficult to be in control of a sale.

During my younger days, I fought against whatever was causing stress. The more difficult the situation, the more intense I became. Ironically, my approach often backfired. Becoming more serious usually made the situation worse and the onset of stress turned into a self-fulfilling prophecy.

Prospects and customers want to deal with salespeople who are highly professional, but they also want someone who is easy to work with and down-to-earth. Maintaining this balance requires a certain amount of patience and self-control, some of which comes naturally from maturity and experience. The rest must be a conscious decision on your part to lighten up. I guess it depends on what you believe. I believe that prospects and customers are almost always more attracted to someone who can laugh at themselves, rather than a person who takes themselves too seriously.

Sometimes, we just need a good dose of perspective. I remember some advice my friend Jack Neel gave me back in college about how to deal with stress. It was 1980 and the government was about to reinstate mandatory draft registration for the military. I remember feeling traumatized by the thought of having to sign my life away in the draft.

Jack said, "Tom, you don't need to worry about registering for the draft because there's only a 50% chance you would ever be drafted. Even if you are drafted, you still don't have to worry, because there's only a 50% chance a war would break out while you served."

"If there isn't a war," Jack continued, "you don't have to worry. Even if there is a war, you still don't have to worry, because there is only a 50% chance you would ever see combat."

"If you never see combat," Jack persisted, "you don't have to worry. Even if you do see combat, you still don't have to worry, because there's only a 50% chance you would ever be shot."

"If you don't get shot, you don't have to worry. Even if you do get shot, you still don't have to worry," Jack added, "because there's only a 50% chance you would die."

"And if you don't die, you don't have to worry. Even if you do die in battle, you still don't have to worry…because you'd be dead."

I offer Jack's advice as a way to suggest that the best way to deal with life's challenges may be to take ourselves less seriously, and even lighten up a little. So, maybe you shouldn't worry…because there's only a 50% chance that stress would adversely affect your health and well-being.

Lesson 97
Pay Attention to Your Rolodex

Harvey Mackay, in his book, *Dig Your Well Before You Are Thirsty*, stresses the importance of having a good network. Essentially, he reinforces the thinking that being successful in business is largely a function of *who* you know, rather than just what you know.

But what does Harvey Mackay know about your situation? He doesn't know your background or your experience. He doesn't know your personality or all the trials and tribulations you've had to suffer through to get where you are today. Consequently, shouldn't we discount his advice on the grounds that he doesn't understand your unique circumstances?

Maybe you should ignore all the experts and do your own research. If you know someone who has been particularly successful in your field, as most of us do, then invest a few moments to ask their advice. Make an appointment if you must, but find a way to spend some time with a "winner" in your field. The best advice comes from those who have already blazed a trail to success, and they are usually more than willing to share their insights.

Early in my career at Shared Medical Systems (SMS), I was fortunate enough to be invited to Jim Macaleer's house for dinner. This wasn't just any dinner, however. Mr. Macaleer was the Chairman of the Board at SMS, and there I was, having dinner with his family. Since it wasn't your basic business dinner, the conversation touched on all kinds of interesting topics. We talked about tennis, cigars, fishing trips, and the finer points of golf. Later, we retired to the open-air patio for an after-dinner drink and I had an opportunity to ask Mr. Macaleer for some business advice. "Jim," I said (hoping that since we had shared a meal, I wasn't stepping too far out of bounds by using his first name), "given your success in business, if you were to give a budding young salesperson one piece of advice, what would that be?"

Mr. Macaleer thoughtfully considered my question and then glanced over at me with a hint of a smile. He explained that business was a team sport, and one person's success often depends on the people with whom they associate. Therefore, he encouraged me to invest in building a network and maintaining personal relationships with people who might be able to contribute to my success down the road.

> Networking is critical to a salesperson's success. Therefore, you must invest in building relationships that will provide value both now and into the future.

I had a similar experience with Enzo Torressi, President of NetFrame Systems. One day after a corporate outing, I approached Enzo and asked him the same question. "Enzo," I said. "Given your experience and success, what one kernel of wisdom would you give an up-and-coming salesperson like myself?"

Without hesitation, Enzo turned to me and said, "Pay attention to your Rolodex."

Ironically, everyone I've asked over the years seems to say the same basic thing—networking is critical to a salesperson's success. Therefore, you must invest in building relationships that will provide value both now and into the future. Perhaps

Harvey Mackay was right. Maybe we should be proactive with regard to networking and start digging our wells before we get thirsty.

Lesson 98
Remember: Amateurs Built the Ark

At the end of the day, there is no substitute for sales experience. Those sellers who have it, have a tremendous advantage. Salespeople who don't have experience, however, face a formidable challenge, especially when they have to compete against seasoned veterans.

Veteran salespeople are able to draw on their previous experiences to give them a mental blueprint for how best to proceed with the sale. They also know to watch out for different obstacles and pitfalls that can cause problems over the course of the sales process. They have essentially learned what to say, when to say it, and when to shut up.

So, if it turns out that you have less experience than one of your competitors in a prospect account, should you just give up? Ironically, many sellers do just that. They let their competitor's experience be a source of intimidation, and they throttle down their own selling efforts to avoid making a mistake. Here's the fallacy with this thinking. If your lack of experience is one of the obstacles standing between you and a successful sale, you should be throttling up your selling efforts.

Experience is an important quality for a salesperson to possess, but so are other qualities like determination, integrity, vigor, humility, and *chutzpah*. Since very few competitive salespeople are perfect in every way, your task is to overcome any potential lack of experience by demonstrating that you have other qualities that are just as important. Many sales are awarded to the salesperson with the most desire, not just the one with the most experience.

> Many sales are awarded to the salesperson with the most desire, not just the one with the most experience.

Truth be told, every successful person on this planet started out with no experience. Steven Spielberg, arguably the most successful filmmaker of all time, started his career as a rookie member of a film crew with no experience. Tiger Woods had very little professional golf experience when he won his first major championship by obliterating the rest of the field at the 1998 Masters. People like John Glenn, Frank Sinatra, Sean Connery, Oprah Winfrey, Walter Cronkite, Elton John, Lee Iacocca, Norman Schwartzkopf, Lance Armstrong, and Donald Trump all started their careers with no experience.

The question you have to answer is, does a lack of experience intimidate you or heighten your resolve to succeed? I would submit that people who succeed do so largely because they have learned how to channel their limitations into a source of energy, rather than a debilitating factor. One could even argue that being the underdog in an account has some unique advantages. After all, isn't it true that amateurs built the ark, while the Titanic was constructed by experienced professionals?

Lesson 99
Always Question the Status Quo

During the preparations for a Thanksgiving feast, the woman of the house took out the dinner ham, cut off both ends, and placed it in the pan. "Why did you just cut off both ends of the ham?" asked her curious daughter.

"I always cut off both ends of the ham. That's what my mother used to do," the woman replied.

"Why did grandma do that?" the daughter persisted.

"I assume she cut off both ends because that was the best way to prepare a ham," the mother answered.

Since the grandmother was there for Thanksgiving, the girl went into the adjacent room and asked, "Grandma, when you prepared a ham, why did you always cut off both ends?"

"Because that's what my mother always did," the grandmother replied.

"Why did she do that?" the girl continued.

"Honestly, I don't know," the grandmother said. "But since your great-grandmother is in the parlor just a few steps away, why don't you go ask her?"

The girl, the mother, and the grandmother walked into the next room to see if great-grandmother could solve the mystery about the proper way to prepare a ham. "Great-grandmother," they asked, "why was it that you always cut off both ends of the ham at Thanksgiving?"

"Oh, that's easy," the great-grandmother said. "I cut off both ends of the ham because my pan was too small."

I have caught myself many times doing whatever was most familiar or most convenient, rather than most effective. One experience that stands out in my mind occurred very early in my professional career when I was implementing hospital information systems for Shared Medical Systems. Midway through one of my largest installation projects, SMS announced a company-wide reorganization, and a manager named Randy Meeks became my new boss.

Randy was a soft-spoken, all-around good guy, that is…until he stuck his nose into my project. Randy didn't offer much advice. He just asked questions. Lots of questions! He asked about the project plan. He asked about the volume of resources that we needed to complete the project. Then, he starting asking why my dates didn't match up with the hospital's staffing projections. He asked what my contingency plans were in the event of a power failure. He even asked why Loxley Thomas, Digital Equipment Corporation's field engineer, was reconfiguring the internal bus of the mainframe computer. Huh?

Frankly, I didn't know the answers to many of Randy's questions, so I did the next best thing. I got upset. "Who does Randy Meeks think he is to show up and start questioning my project?" I fumed. After several grueling days of non-stop questions, Randy left the project site, with a plan to return in two weeks. "I'll show him," I thought to myself!

For the next two weeks, I had everyone on the project working double time to make sure every base was covered, and no stone was left unturned. I personally worked nights and weekends and took hundreds of pages of notes. I was going to show Randy Meeks that he didn't need to check behind me.

Randy showed up two weeks later and he started asking questions, but this time I was ready. My whole team was ready. When Randy asked a question, we gave him a detailed response. In fact, we not only answered his questions, we had all the possible scenarios laid out, and we even had contingency plans ready in the event something went wrong. For the duration of the project, we made it a goal to stay one step ahead of Randy Meeks' questions. And, darn it, that's exactly what we did.

After the project was over, Randy took the entire project team out to dinner for a celebration. While we were sitting around a large table, Randy leaned over to me and asked, "Tom, what would you say was the key to your success in this project?" Suddenly, it hit me. Much of our success was due to Randy's willingness to challenge the status quo, by asking the hard questions. In doing so, Randy taught us that it was better to investigate new alternatives than to be complacent with our current level of ignorance. For me, it was one of life's golden lessons. In fact, as I thought back on the project, once we did start challenging the status quo, by asking our own questions, it was amazing how much we didn't know. Come to think of it, Randy Meeks' influence is probably the reason I have been asking lots of questions ever since.

Experiences like this make me wonder how many salespeople 'cut off both ends of their ham' just because that's the way they've always done it. Perhaps that's what their sales manager has always done too. Maybe that's how they did it in a previous job. In any case, it's very possible that the status quo could actually be one of your greatest adversaries.

Today's selling environment is rapidly changing. Your competitors are getting smarter, and everyone is having to adjust to an evolving business landscape. If you want to be successful as a sales professional, both now and into the future, then you must change too, which means challenging the status quo. Perhaps you can start by stepping outside the box of traditional sales thinking and implementing the ideas and strategies that were introduced in this book.

If you are going to challenge the status quo, have fun and be creative. Make some mistakes, and try not to be overwhelmed by the size of the challenge. Ask lots of questions. Do something different. Remember: someone is going to win the sale, so that person might as well be you. The good news is, you don't have to win by much...*because it only takes one percent to have a competitive edge in sales.*

Lesson 100
The Best Way to Eat an Elephant

Congratulations! You made it to the last chapter in the book. This means you are either very bored and have nothing better to do with your time, or you have committed yourself to excellence in the profession of selling. I'm guessing it's the latter.

As we wrap things up, I want to leave you with some thoughts about implementation—the most important part of any sales methodology. Once the concepts get communicated, these ideas must then be put into motion and integrated into your daily routine. This is ultimately where the rubber meets the road, as they say.

Implementation can be an exciting phase of the learning process. I do realize, however, that the thought of integrating 100 chapters of conceptual material into your daily routine can be an overwhelming task to say the least. Believe me, the thought of having to write 100 chapters was just as daunting. Nevertheless, I fulfilled my destiny, and you can succeed in fulfilling yours.

Whether you are excited about implementing new strategies and techniques or you are feeling a bit overwhelmed, there an old adage that says: "The best way to eat an elephant...is one bite at a time."

Oddly enough, I have learned that it's impossible to write a book all at once. If you sit down in front of a blank piece of paper with the intention of writing a whole book, you will most likely fail. It is possible, however, to write a sentence. It is also possible to group multiple sentences together into paragraphs, and multiple paragraphs into sections. Over time, sections turn into chapters, and so on. That's how you write a book, one bite (or sentence) at a time.

Though we have covered a lot of information in this book, and in *Secrets of Question Based Selling*, my objective was not to overwhelm you. I simply wanted to give you many ideas that you can use to differentiate yourself and your solutions in an increasingly competitive business environment. Once you have a vision for how each of these concepts can enhance your performance, you can start to induce change and improve your strategic sales process—one step at a time.

Be assured that your momentum will snowball as you implement these lessons. With each one-percent idea achieving a positive result, it makes it easier to implement the next idea... and the next. Then, it's just a matter of desire for how quickly you want to take your career to the next level.

Bonus Chapter
Always, Always, Always...
Ask for Referrals

Word-of-mouth is the best form of advertising and customer referrals will always be worth their weight in commission checks. But there are two ways to leverage referrals that will create new business. One is to simply satisfy your customer base and hope they spread the word. The other is to proactively ask for referrals.

When you do a particularly good job for one of your customers, you earn the right to ask for referrals. But don't be covert about it. Customers know that you want to grow your business. It's more effective to just come right out and say, "Mr. Prospect, my business is ultimately driven by word-of-mouth. Therefore, I would like to ask for your help. Do you know anyone else in your company, or in other organizations, who would benefit from knowing about our solutions?" Depending on the circumstance, you can also ask for contact information and offer to follow up. You can even ask customers to make the introduction for you to help boost your credibility with new contacts. However it happens, you can leverage your success and increase your sales pipeline by taking the initiative when it comes to asking for referrals.

In that vein, I would like to ask for *your* help. Word-of-mouth is critical in my business too. So, if there are others in your organization, or in your circle of contacts, who would benefit from this book, or from Question Based Selling, then I will practice what I preach and thank you in advance for spreading the word.

About the Author

Thomas A. Freese is an internationally-known author, speaker, and trainer—but first and foremost, Tom is a salesman. Having spent the bulk of his professional career in the trenches of sales and management, Tom became frustrated with the fact that most of the sales training programs that are being delivered today were developed 20+ years ago. He found it especially odd that corporations would embrace this material given the significant changes that have occurred in the selling environment over the last twenty years. Over time, Tom became convinced that "standard" sales training courses tend to turn out salespeople who all sound the same. The problem is, if your salespeople sound just like everyone else, they forfeit their competitive edge. This realization started Tom's quest to develop a different approach.

Freese's first book, *Secrets of Question Based Selling*, has been heralded as one of the most innovative and down-to-earth sales books ever written. In this, his second book, *It Only Takes 1% to Have a Competitive Edge in Sales*, Tom builds on the concepts he introduced in the QBS Methodology to show salespeople and sales organizations how they can differentiate themselves and their solutions in an increasingly competitive marketplace.

When Tom is not out training salespeople and sales organizations all over the world, he gravitates to a simpler life, living in Atlanta with his wife, Laura, and two daughters, Sarah and Mary Claire.

Contact Information

More information about QBS and the sales training programs we deliver is available at:

QBS Research, Inc.
PO Box 922933
Atlanta, Georgia 30010-2933
Ofc: (770) 840-7640
Fax: (770) 840-7642
Email: info@QBSresearch.com

www.QBSresearch.com